PREVAILING PRAYER TO PEACE

PREVAILING PRAYER TO PEACE

Kenneth E. Hagin

Sixth Printing • 1978

Kenneth Hagin Ministries
P.O. Box 50126
Tulsa, Oklahoma 74150

ISBN 0-89276-071-0

ISBN 0-89276-071-0

Contents

FOREWORD

PRAYER is joining forces with God the Father. It is fellowshiping with Him. It is carrying out His will upon the earth. John Wesley, founder of Methodism, said, "It seems that God is limited by our prayer life. He can do nothing for humanity unless someone asks Him to do it."

"Why is this?" you might ask. You see, God made the world and the fullness thereof. Then He made Man and gave Man dominion over all the work of His hands. Adam was the god of this world. Adam, however, committed high treason and sold out to Satan. Then Satan became the god of this world. He is called that in the New Testament (II Cor. 4:4). God doesn't just move in on top of Satan. If He did, then Satan could accuse God of doing the same thing he had done. But—God has devised a plan of salvation and sent His Son, the Lord Jesus Christ, whom Satan could not and did not touch. Through Jesus, God redeemed Mankind! Now authority has been restored to us through Jesus Christ and when we ask God—then He can move! That is why it seems He can do nothing unless someone asks Him to do it. It is of utmost importance that believers know how to pray.

THE AUTHOR

ABOUT THE AUTHOR

The ministry of Rev. Kenneth Hagin is known around the world as a Ministry based on faith. A strong emphasis of his ministry is the independence and authority of the believer to reach God in the time of need. He has been in the full-time ministry since 1936, pastoring for 12 years. He is the author of several books and a well-known speaker at many conferences and seminars throughout the nation.

PREVAILING PRAYER TO PEACE

*By faith we reach out to claim that which we need
and thereby create the reality of it in our life.*

Seven Steps to Answered Prayer
(Part I)

James 1:6–8; Joshua 1:8
Matthew 7:7–8; Mark 11:23–24

A s we begin this series of studies on the subject of prayer, the first two lessons will deal with the fundamental aspects of praying that get results. If the believer will faithfully follow these steps in prayer, he can be sure of an answer.

Step 1: Decide What You Want From God

JAMES 1:6–8

6 But let him ask in faith, nothing wavering. For he that wavereth is like a wave of the sea driven with the wind and tossed.

7 For let not that man think that he shall receive any thing of the Lord.

8 A double minded man is unstable in all his ways.

The above scriptures show us the importance of decisiveness. James said that if a man wavers, if he cannot make up his mind, he is "unstable in all his ways" and cannot expect to "receive any thing of the Lord."

So many times we are indefinite in our praying. When I have asked people what they are praying about, they sometimes answer that they don't know. One person said that he was praying just to be praying. Of course, there is one kind of prayer in which we pray to worship and have fellowship with God. But in this lesson we are dealing primarily with praying to get an answer to our prayers.

And if we are not careful, this general type of praying will carry over when we need to be specific about a certain need.

If you went to a grocery store and pushed your cart up and down the aisles without buying anything, people would think something was wrong with you. But if you send a child to buy certain items and he buys just those things, then he is being definite. The same is true with praying. It would be better to pray for two or three minutes and know what you are praying about than to pray aimlessly for two or three hours. Decide what you want from God and be definite about it.

Step 2: Read Scriptures That Promise the Answer You Need

JOSHUA 1:8

8 This book of the law shall not depart out of thy mouth; but thou shalt meditate therein day and night, that thou mayest observe to do according to all that is written therein: for then thou shalt make thy way prosperous, and then thou shalt have good success.

In order to be successful in our prayer life, God's Word must be foremost. As we feed upon His Word we build this into our inner consciousness. Then in time of need we are prepared and can use the appropriate scriptures against the devil when he tries to make us doubt God and rob us of what we want.

When in the wilderness Satan tempted Jesus to turn the stones into bread, Jesus answered with the Word. He said, "It is written, That man shall not live by bread alone, but by every word of God." Then Satan took Him upon an exceedingly high mountain and showed Him all the kingdoms of the world. He told Jesus that if He would fall down and worship him, he would give all these kingdoms to Him. Again Jesus answered, ". . . It is written, Thou shalt worship the Lord thy God, and him only shalt thou serve." Satan then took Him upon a pinnacle of the temple and said to Him, "Cast thyself down." Again Jesus answered with the Word saying, "It is said, Thou shalt not tempt the Lord thy God" (Luke 4:3-12).

Jesus did not use a single weapon to defeat the devil other than that which believers have today—the Word of God. All we have to do in the face of temptation and doubt is to say, "It is written." If the scriptures are firmly implanted in our heart, we are prepared for any attacks of the devil.

In matters of guidance, search the scriptures to see what God has to say about any situation. His Word plainly shows us His will. If the scriptures don't promise us what we may be seeking, then we don't have any business praying for it. We should not want anything that the Word of God says we shouldn't have. On the other hand, when praying for things that are expressly promised in the Word, we can have complete confidence that God will give us what we need. Years ago I wrote in red ink on the fly leaf of my Bible, "The Bible says it, I believe it, and that settles it!"

Many people try to pray beyond their faith. It is the Word of God that gives faith. "So then faith cometh by hearing, and hearing by the word of God" (Romans 10:17). The reason that people do not pray with confidence and faith is that they do not know the scriptures well enough to know if what they are praying for is God's will. They may *hope* it is, but they don't *know* it is. As we read God's Word and learn His will, we can appropriate His promises for our every need.

Step 3: Ask God for the Things You Want

MATTHEW 7:7-8

7 Ask, and it shall be given you; seek, and ye shall find; knock, and it shall be opened unto you:

8 For every one that asketh receiveth; and he that seeketh findeth; and to him that knocketh it shall be opened.

In Matthew 6:8 Jesus said, ". . . Your Father knoweth what things ye have need of, before ye ask him." Yet in the next chapter He tells us to ask Him for our needs as we see in the verses quoted above. Therefore, even though He knows our needs, He wants us to bring them to Him and ask His help.

Step 4: Believe That You Receive

MARK 11:23-24

23 For verily I say unto you, That whosoever shall say unto this mountain, Be thou removed, and be thou cast into the sea; and shall not doubt in his heart, but shall believe that those things which he saith shall come to pass; he shall have whatsoever he saith.

24 Therefore I say unto you, What things soever ye desire, when ye pray, believe that ye receive them, and ye shall have them.

The Amplified version of the above verse says, "When you pray, trust and be confident that it is granted you, and you'll get it." You've got to believe you have it before you get it.

To understand this better we need to realize that there are two kinds of truth: sense-knowledge truth and revelation truth. Some people think that truth pertains to things they can see with their physical eye. But we cannot see the things of the Spirit. They are not flesh and they are not material. Everything that we need is provided for us in the spiritual realm. "Blessed be the God and Father of our Lord Jesus Christ, who hath blessed us with all spiritual blessings in heavenly places in Christ" (Eph. 1:3). Everything we need has been provided for us in Christ Jesus. We may not always be able to see them, but they are there.

When "sense-knowledge truth" contradicts "revelation truth," or the Word of God, then I start walking by revelation truth. I walk by what God says. That which is in the spiritual realm is made real in the natural realm through faith. Faith grasps it and creates the reality of it in our life.

Therefore, when you pray believe that you receive that which you are asking for and you shall have it. This is beyond our natural thinking and the natural mind cannot grasp it. But we are to walk by faith and not by sight.

Once while preaching in a small church, I got too warm while preaching and when I stepped outdoors after the service my body was wet with perspiration. When the cold outdoor air hit me in the face, my throat started hurting, and by the time I reached the parking lot I could hardly speak. The next day my chest started hurting and I couldn't speak above a whisper.

I started reading the scriptures on healing. With my Bible opened before me, I prayed silently and said, "Lord, your Word tells me that I am healed. If I asked my body if I were healed, the answer would be no. If I asked my feelings if I were healed, the answer would be no. If I were to ask the people around me if I were healed, they would say that I was not. Your Word says that God is

truth and every man is a liar. So if I say I'm not healed, I am a liar. Your Word says that God cannot lie. Romans 3:4 says, 'God forbid: yea, let God be true, but every man a liar; as it is written, That thou mightest be justified in thy sayings, and mightest overcome when thou are judged'."

When it came time for the evening service, I got up to go preach. Stepping up to the microphone, I said that I wanted to thank God that I was healed. The congregation looked at me as if I were crazy because I was barely whispering. I began to tell them what the Word of God says about healing and showed them from the Word that I was healed. I told them what God says is true and that if I said I wasn't healed, I would be lying. I told them that I wanted them to stand and praise God with me because I was healed. As we stood and began praising God, I hadn't said "Hallelujah" three times until my voice came back. Then I preached my sermon with a strong, clear voice. That night the congregation saw an illustration of faith in action. All we have to do is ask God for the things we want, and believe that we have them. ✞

MEMORY TEXT:

"Ask, and it shall be given you; seek, and ye shall find; knock, and it shall be opened unto you: For every one that asketh receiveth; and he that seeketh findeth; and to him that knocketh it shall be opened." *(Matt. 7:7–8)*

THE LESSON IN ACTION: *"But be ye doers of the word, and not hearers only..."* James 1:22

This week I will put the lesson into practice by doing the following:

Thinking faith thoughts and speaking faith words
leads the heart out of defeat and into victory.

Seven Steps to Answered Prayer
(Part II)

Proverbs 4:20-22
Philippians 4:6

Last week's lesson covered four steps to be taken in order to see our prayers answered:

1. Decide what you want from God.
   a. Be definite in laying your petitions before Him.
2. Read scriptures that promise the answer you need.
   a. Search the Bible for scriptures that apply to your particular need.
   b. With God's Word firmly implanted in your heart, you can be prepared against Satan's attacks.
3. Ask God for the things you want.
   a. Even though He knows what we have need of, it is His divine plan that we make known to Him our wants.
4. Believe that you receive.
   a. A stubborn faith that refuses to look at circumstances produces results.

In this lesson we will deal with three more steps which we can take to pray more effectively.

Step 5: Refuse to Doubt

Let every thought and desire affirm that you have what you ask. Never permit a mental picture of failure to remain in your mind. Never doubt for one minute that you have the answer. If doubts persist, rebuke them. Get your mind on the answer. James 4:7 says, "Resist the devil, and he will flee from you." Doubt is of the devil. Resist it.

Eradicate every image, suggestion, feeling or thought which does not contribute to your faith that you shall have what you ask. Enjoy those things that do contribute to your faith.

When my daughter was three years old a growth appeared in the corner of her left eye. It kept growing larger and larger until it was the size of the end of her little finger. It was a cause for concern. I knew in my spirit that it was going to go away. Friends told us, "Oh, it will probably just go away as she gets older." I knew that when God healed her they would just say that it would have gone away anyway, so I took her to an eye specialist for an examination. He said that she had a type of growth that would never go away without surgery. He suggested that she be operated on soon, as the growth would become larger and larger until eventually it would hang down over her face. I thanked him for his diagnosis and left.

That night about 10:15 I prayed about it and said, "Lord, the doctor said an operation is necessary, but your Word says that 'whatsoever you ask the Father He will give it you.' I am standing on that scripture. I have asked you and now I believe that you have done it. I believe tonight at 10:15 for my baby's healing. I thank you for the healing."

I got up off my knees and as I started to go to bed the devil told me to turn the light on and see if the growth was gone. But immediately I eradicated that suggestion. Several times during the night I was awakened and the suggestion would come to me to go see if the growth was gone yet. I just said, "Satan, why should I get up and turn the light on to see if it's gone yet? I know it's gone because I have God's Word for it."

When I got up the next morning the same suggestion returned, and again I pushed it from my mind. I kept saying that I had received the healing last night at 10:15. When I saw my daughter at breakfast that morning, the growth was still on her eye. But the Bible tells us to walk by faith and not by sight, so I ignored the physical evidence of the growth. I walked by faith and kept thanking God for her healing.

Every time our family gathered at the dinner table, I saw that ugly growth sticking right out at me. I just kept thanking God for the healing which took place that night at 10:15. I was so engrossed in thanking God for the healing that I really don't know when it left. Not long after that we were driving along in the car and my daughter was standing up on the front seat between my wife and me. I turned to say something to my wife and happened to notice that the growth was gone. I mentioned this to my wife and she said that it had been gone for about ten days. We had seen a miracle as a result of believing God and thanking Him for the answer while our physical senses told us it had not happened. This is the realm in which the battle of prayer is fought and won.

Our thoughts are governed by observation, association and teachings. We must guard against every evil thought and every doubt that comes into the mind. We must stay away from all places and things that do not support the affirmation that God has answered prayer. Sometimes this means staying away from churches that teach more doubt than faith. "Finally, brethren, whatsoever things are true, whatsoever things are honest, whatsoever things are just, whatsoever things are pure, whatsoever things are lovely, whatsoever things are of good report; if there be any virtue, and if there be any praise, think on these things" (Phil. 4:8).

Step 6: Meditate on the Promises

PROVERBS 4:20–22

20 My son, attend to my words; incline thine ear unto my sayings.

21 Let them not depart from thine eyes; keep them in the midst of thine heart.

22 For they are life unto those that find them, and health to all their flesh.

Meditate constantly on the promises upon which you based the answer to your prayer. See yourself in possession of what you have asked God for, and make plans accordingly as if it were already a reality. God will make His Word good unto you if you will act upon it.

If God's Word says that He hears and answers prayer, and if that Word doesn't depart from before your eyes, then you are sure to see yourself with the things you asked for. If you don't see yourself with them, then God's Word has departed from before your eyes. If you don't stand by the Word, then even though God wants to stand by you He cannot. The only way God works is through His Word. He moves in line with His Word. He has magnified His Word above His name. If you stand by the Word, God will stand by you.

Many people pray and pray, but they don't pray by the Word. John 15:7 says, "If ye abide in me, and my words abide in you, ye shall ask what ye will, and it shall be done unto you." Jesus didn't just say, "If ye abide in me," He also said, "and my words abide in you." With His words abiding in us, we have ground to stand upon.

One time I went to pray for an elderly lady evangelist in Fort Worth, Texas. Many people had been saved and filled with the Spirit under her ministry. Now, at the age of eighty-two, she had been operated on and found to have seven cancers in her body. The doctors just sewed her back up and told her she didn't have long to live.

Months had come and gone and, though bedfast, she was still alive. When I talked to her she said that she was old enough to die, but we told her to let God heal her first, that if she lived she could still win many more souls to God. Then we read to her Proverbs 4:20–22, the scriptures quoted above, and told her to visualize herself well and preaching.

I saw this woman eight months later and she was out holding evangelistic meetings. She came up to me in one of my services, threw her arms around me and hugged me. It startled me, and then she realized that I didn't recognize her. She looked so different as she had gained weight and appeared in excellent health. She told me that she was so glad that we hadn't let her die. She had done just what we had told her to do. She had begun to picture herself well and now she was out working for God again. She had scheduled evangelistic meetings for the entire summer.

I later heard that this woman lived to be ninety-one years old. She didn't die of cancer, but had many more fruitful years for the Master. Before her healing she had visualized herself dead. But we got her to see herself with what God had provided for her. We have to see ourselves with what we have asked for.

Step 7: Give God the Praise

PHILIPPIANS 4:6

6 Be careful for nothing; but in every thing by prayer and supplication with thanksgiving let your requests be made known unto God.

The words "be careful for nothing" mean "in nothing be anxious." It means, "Do not fret or have any anxiety about anything." As long as we fret and are anx-

ious, praying and fasting won't do any good. This verse says "with thanksgiving," and this comes after praying about the matter. We thank God for the answer after we have prayed for it. Therefore, the final step to answered prayer is to lift your heart to God constantly in gratitude and increasing praise for what He has done and for what He is doing for you now.

Make every prayer concerning what you have asked for a statement of faith and praise instead of unbelief. You can say that you do have faith as easily as you can think thoughts of doubt and unbelief. It is thinking faith thoughts and speaking faith words that leads the heart out of defeat and into victory. Do not accept defeat. Do not be denied. It is your family right, your redemption right, to have what God has promised. It is yours and it will come, so accept it and it will become a reality.

Andrew Murray said, "It is not good taste to ask God for the same thing over and over again. If, when you do pray again, what you've prayed for hasn't materialized, don't pray for it again in the same way because that would be unbelief. Remind God that you asked for it and what His Word says, and tell Him that you are expecting it. Then thank Him for it." Many times people undo their prayers. They get into unbelief and stay there as if they are spinning their wheels.

During a convention in Texas I heard Raymond T. Richey lead in prayer for a man who was in the hospital dying. After we prayed, we thanked God that He had

---

According to I John 4:4 the Greater One lives in me. He is greater than Satan, greater than demons or evil spirits, greater than sickness or disease. He is greater than any force I may come against and He lives in me!

heard us. Brother Richey started to walk away from the pulpit, but then turned around and went back to the microphone. He asked how many in the congregation were going to keep praying for this man in the hospital. Nearly everyone raised his hand." What do you want to do that for?" he asked. "We have already prayed for him. Now let us keep praising God because He has healed that man."

At the close of the service someone came in and announced that the man who had been dying had suddenly revived and was going to be all right. He had seen Jesus walk into his room and He had said, "I am the Lord that healeth thee." Although unconscious, the man woke up and immediately was well. This had happened while we had been praying.

The Christian man or woman who will practice these seven steps to answered prayer will discover great victory in his prayer life.

MEMORY TEXT:

"If ye abide in me, and my words abide in you, ye shall ask what ye will, and it shall be done unto you."

(John 15:7)

THE LESSON IN ACTION: *"But be ye doers of the word, and not hearers only..."* James 1:22

This week I will put the lesson into practice by doing the following:

Lesson 3

The Prayer That Unlocks Heaven

John 16:23-24; Ephesians 5:20

When we go to our automobile, we have a key that unlocks the door. We may say that we unlock the door, but really it is the key that does it. We have a key that fits the ignition. We couldn't start the car without that key. The key is the important factor in driving that car. We could get nowhere without it.

There is a key to prayer without which we can get nowhere. This key will unlock the doors and windows of heaven and grant our every need. We read about this key in John 16:23-24.

The Name of Jesus

JOHN 16:23-24

23 And in that day ye shall ask me nothing. Verily, verily, I say unto you, whatsoever ye shall ask the Father in my name, he will give it you.

24 Hitherto have ye asked nothing in my name: ask, and ye shall receive, that your joy may be full.

Jesus is our Mediator, Intercessor, Advocate and Lord. He stands between us and the Father. In no place in the Bible is it recorded that Jesus told His disciples to pray to Him. They were always told to pray to the Father in His name. Therefore, if we wish to be sure of our prayers reaching the throne, we must come according to the rules laid down in the Word of God.

In the scripture quoted above notice that Jesus said, "In that day ye shall ask me nothing." He said this before He went away and was talking about the mediatorial session at the right hand of the Father when He ascends and is seated. Another translation reads, "In that day ye shall not pray to me." Jesus said to ask the Father in His name. This is the key that will unlock heaven in our behalf.

We can tell Jesus how much we love Him, but when it comes to praying and asking, we must ask the Father through the Lord Jesus. We read in Ephesians 3:14-15, "For this cause I bow my knees unto the Father of our Lord Jesus Christ, Of whom the whole family in heaven and earth is named." It is not important which church we belong to, but it is important which family we belong to.

Overflowing Joy

John 16:24 says, ". . . Ask, and ye shall receive, that your joy may be full." There is real joy in knowing that the Father will answer our prayers.

The beloved preacher Smith Wigglesworth worked for many years as a plumber before he began his full-time preaching ministry. One time while installing plumbing in a large house, he noticed that the lady of the house kept coming in, looking around and then leaving. Finally she came in, sat down beside where he was working and asked, "What in the world is it that causes that wonderful expression on your face? You look as if you are full of joy."

He told her that that morning at breakfast his wife had told him that two of their children were very ill. Before they ate, they went upstairs, laid hands on the children and prayed for them, and they were instantly healed. Then they came

17

downstairs with their parents and joined them for breakfast. Wigglesworth said that it was so wonderful to have such a wonderful Jesus.

He told her that the scripture says, "Ask, and ye shall receive, that your joy may be full." Certainly our joy could not be full if our children were ill. But the Lord told us to ask Him for what we need, "that your joy may be full."

The woman asked Wigglesworth if Jesus would save her also and give her this wonderful joy. Wigglesworth told her that she too could be saved and experience this peace and joy, and while she was standing there she accepted the Lord. She was happy and rejoicing, and asked him if she would keep this joy. He answered that the only way to keep it was to give it away. He told her that she should tell all the women in her club meeting about her salvation. She did and all of them were saved. This is the way to keep it—tell about it.

If when Wigglesworth went to work he had had two sick children at home, his joy could not have been full. He would have been worried. He would have looked distressed. Instead he had a light on his face, a radiance that was obvious to all who saw him. Something seemed to be flowing out of him. What was it? It was the joy that the Father has promised when we ask Him for our needs and receive in faith.

On another occasion Wigglesworth was in dire financial circumstances. At the time he was in London visiting in the home of a wealthy man. Wigglesworth simply committed his financial burden to the Lord and refused to worry about it. He knew the Lord would take care of it.

While he and his friend were out walking in the park, Wigglesworth was happy and was singing as they walked along. He didn't mention his need to his friend, for He had committed it to the Lord.

Instead he was happy and rejoicing in his spirit. His friend commented that he would give all he owned just to have the same spirit of joy that Wigglesworth had. Wigglesworth told him that it wouldn't cost him anything. All he had to do was cast all his cares on Jesus. He explained that this was what he had done, and without a care in the world, he could now be free and happy. He did not mention to his friend his financial need, but instead talked of victory and joy in Christ Jesus. One man had material wealth but no joy. The other lacked for material things but was filled with joy. What was the secret? Wigglesworth knew the truth of the scripture, "Ask, and ye shall receive, that your joy may be full."

Can your joy be full if you have great financial burdens pressing you? Can your joy be full if you have unpaid bills that are due? If you have committed these needs to the Lord, if you have asked Him to supply your needs, and believe that "ye shall receive," then your joy can be full.

Joy That Precedes the Fact

Sometimes you have to have the joy before you will have what you are praying for. If you are worrying and trying to figure matters out alone, you hinder God from helping you, for then you are carrying the burden instead of letting Him carry it. In fact, if you are worrying about them, it will do little good to pray, for you are not praying in faith. "Be careful for nothing; but in every thing by prayer and supplication with thanksgiving let your requests be made known unto God. And the peace of God, which passeth all understanding, shall keep your hearts and minds through Christ Jesus" (Phil. 4:6-7).

My mother once told me that when she knew I was traveling she prayed that the Lord would be with me. While traveling on the road in evangelistic meetings, often when I would finish a meeting in California, I would get in the car and drive straight through to my home in Tulsa without stopping until I got there. She said she stayed awake at night waiting for the telephone to ring. I told her that she was wasting her time to pray then. There was no need to pray and ask the Lord to protect me if she was going to stay awake worrying.

Prayer means more than that. "Ask, and ye shall receive, that your joy may be full," We are full of joy even before the thing we have asked for materializes because we know He heard us. We have His Word.

Ephesians 5:20

20 Giving thanks always for all things unto God and the Father in the name of our Lord Jesus Christ.

Notice here that Paul tells us that we are to give thanks always for all things in the name of Jesus "unto God and the Father." Paul tells us expressly that we are to pray to the Father and not to Jesus. In all of our real praise and thanksgiving the name of Jesus is the access to the heart of the Father. When you wish to get an answer to your prayers, follow the teachings of the Word.

Someone has said that the way in which we pray doesn't make much difference. But if it made no difference, why would God have inspired Paul to write his epistles as he did? To say that these verses are not important would make as

According to Philippians 4:13 (The Amplified Bible) I have strength for all things in Christ Who empowers me—I am ready for anything and equal to anything through Him Who infuses inner strength into me (that is, I am self-sufficient in Christ's sufficiency).

much sense as it would to say that John 3:16 isn't important. If we believe that John 3:16 is important, then we must also believe that all scriptures are important and are for our instruction in our walk with God. When you wish to get an answer to your prayers, follow the teachings of the Lord and pray to the Father in the name of Jesus.

When many people pray they conclude their prayer, "for Jesus' sake." However, we are not told in the Word to pray for Jesus' sake. We are taught to pray in the name of Jesus. What is the difference? If you were to go to the bank and ask the cashier to cash a check for a friend, he would ask you if you have an account there with money enough to guarantee this check. If you haven't, the cashier would not cash the check. But if you came with a check for a man who had an account in that bank, you would be able to cash the check. The same is true when we go to God and tell Him to do something for Jesus' sake. We are asking that it be done to help Jesus and on our credit. If I had a stomach ache and I ask God to heal me for Jesus' sake, that is foolish. It is my stomach that hurts. I don't want to be healed for Him. We are the ones who need the help. He has the standing or credit, and we can come in His name.

It makes a lot of difference what our outlook and attitude is. The reason that we fail many times in our praying is that our approach is all wrong. Sometimes we think that because of our own merit, or our own goodness, God should answer our prayers. When Peter and John had ministered to the lame man at the Gate Beautiful, as recording in the third chapter of Acts, the people who were gathered around were amazed and thought that it was through some special power of these men that the lame man was healed. But Peter said, ". . . Why look ye so earnestly on us, as though by our own power or holiness we had made this man to walk?"

(Acts 3:12). It isn't by our own power or holiness that we get an answer to prayer. We don't get our prayers answered because we are good. They are answered because of Jesus. He has a standing in heaven. He is the only approach to the Father. We cannot get there any other way. It is in His name that we can come.

Jesus gave us the right and the authority to use His name. The key to seeing answers to our prayers is through the mighty name of Jesus.

THE LESSON IN ACTION: *"But be ye doers of the word, and not hearers only..."* James 1:22

This week I will put the lesson into practice by doing the following:

Jesus gave us the power of attorney, the right to use His name.

Lesson 4

The Authority of Jesus' Name

Mark 16:17-18

God hears and answers prayer. We might as well settle that. It works. Too much of the time people just make a stab in the dark at praying. They call it praying and let it go at that. They hope that something works out some way or somehow. But we need to take our stand on God's Word and let heaven, hell and earth know that God's Word is true and that we believe it.

We need to be able to grow in prayer. Many times God condescends to meet us on an elementary level, but it is better when we can grow spiritually and meet Him on His level. The Bible teaches that there is a similarity between physical growth and spiritual growth. "As newborn babes, desire the sincere milk of the word, that ye may grow thereby" (I Peter 2:2). No one is born a fully grown adult. We are born as babies and grow up. No one is born a fully grown Christian. Christians are newborn babes and then grow up. As we mature in the Word, we should be able to improve our prayer life.

When I was a child I prayed, "Now I lay me down to sleep . . ." but I don't pray that way anymore. I've grown beyond that. When we were spiritual babes we might have prayed certain ways, but God wants us to grow spiritually. God will require more of us now than He did even a few years ago. When light comes and teaching is given, God requires us to walk in the light of it.

Believers' Rights in the Name of Jesus

MARK 16:17-18

17 And these signs shall follow them that believe; In my name shall they cast out devils; they shall speak with new tongues;

18 They shall take up serpents; and if they drink any deadly thing, it shall not hurt them; they shall lay hands on the sick, and they shall recover.

In our last lesson we studied Christ's teachings, found in John 16:23-24, concerning the fact that prayer should be addressed to the Father in Jesus' name. We saw that this is the key to seeing our prayers answered. In this lesson we will look at the rights we have in Jesus' name.

Jesus gave us the power of attorney, or the right to use His name, not only in praying for our individual needs, but also in dealing with the devil. He said, "In my name shall they cast out devils . . ." When Jesus appointed the seventy disciples and sent them forth, "The seventy returned again with joy, saying, Lord, even the devils are subject unto us through thy name" (Luke 10:17). In Acts 16:16-18 we read where Paul cast an evil spirit out of a girl. "But Paul, being grieved, turned and said to the spirit, I command thee in the name of Jesus Christ to come out of her. And he came out the same hour."

I once knew of a lady whose daughter was in a mental institution. This mother decided to pray the prayer of faith for her daughter, to exercise her authority in Jesus' name, and cast the devil out that kept her daughter bound. She asked twelve women, whom she knew to be women of strong faith, to go with her to the mental institution to pray for her daughter.

When they arrived, the woman told the attendant that she wanted to see her daughter. When they arrived at the padded cell where the woman was being held, the mother said to the attendant, "I want you to open the door and let me in there because I want to pray for my daughter."

"You can't do that," he answered. "She'll kill you. She is violently insane." He argued that he couldn't let her in, that he would lose his job, but all the time he was unlocking the door. The woman stepped in and he locked the door again.

In the padded cell was a woman who looked more like an animal than a human. Her hair had grown long, her nails were grown out, and she hissed and spit at them as an animal would.

While the twelve ladies prayed silently, the mother prayed, commanding the devil to come out of her daughter in the name of Jesus. She prayed like this for about ten minutes. Suddenly the daughter relaxed, looked up, and said, "Mama! Is that you, Mama?" She threw her arms around her and hugged and kissed her. That day she was dismissed from the institution as being well. This mother knew her rights, she knew the authority that was hers to cast out devils in Jesus' name.

Jesus also said in the seventeenth verse of the above passage, "In my name . . . they shall speak with new tongues." Every believer has the right and can speak with tongues.

The next verse says that in Jesus' name "they shall take up serpents; and if they drink any deadly thing, it shall not hurt them." This doesn't mean, of course, that we are to take up serpents and handle them just to try to prove something. It means that if we are accidentally bitten, as Paul was on the island of Malta, we can shake off the serpent and claim immunity in the name of Jesus.

We read in Acts 28:3-6 of how when Paul was shipwrecked and picked up some sticks to build a fire, a viper came out and fastened on his hand. The people who saw this expected him to fall dead at any moment. When he didn't die, become sick or his hand even become swollen, the people knew they had witnessed a miracle.

I have heard of similar experiences in our day. A woman missionary in a foreign country was stung by a deadly scorpion. There was no antidote for the bite in those days, and its sting was always fatal. No one had ever been known to live. The missionary was out on the street when the scorpion stung her, and people watching expected her to swell up and die. But she just shook it off in Jesus' name and didn't even get sick to her stomach. As a result many of those people were saved.

The scripture further says, "And if they drink any deadly thing, it shall not hurt them." Again, this doesn't mean that we can drink something poisonous just to try to prove a point. It means that if we do accidentally, we can claim immunity in the name of the Lord Jesus Christ.

A number of years ago a religious denomination was holding a convention in Corpus Christi, Texas. After the people began to gather at the grounds where they were having the convention, some of them began to fall ill. Soon about twenty or thirty people were desperately sick, and they began praying for one another.

As they prayed, someone had a revelation that the water in one of the hotels was poisoned. This was in the days when they didn't have running water, but had a pitcher and bowl on a wash stand in each room. This person cautioned the rest of the people not to drink any more water. The Lord answered prayer and everyone was healed. No one even had to have his stomach pumped.

They took a sample of the water to a nearby naval station. Laboratory tests showed that there was enough poison in the water to kill a regiment of men. Under such circumstances we have a right to claim immunity in Jesus' name.

Jesus then said, "They shall lay hands on the sick, and they shall recover" (Verse 18). Don't lay hands on someone and say, "If it be the Lord's will . . ." Lay your hands on them and claim their deliverance in the name of Jesus. You have solid ground to stand upon.

Let me point out that Jesus said, "In my name . . ." It is in His name that we can cast out devils. It is in His name that we can speak with new tongues. It is in His name that we can claim immunity if we accidentally take up serpents or drink any deadly thing. It is in His name that we can lay hands on the sick, and they shall recover. It is His name that gives us authority to claim these things.

Notice also He said that *we* lay hands on the sick. We do the laying on of hands, not Jesus, not the Holy Ghost. We lay hands on the sick person in Jesus' name. By the same token, we are the ones who talk in tongues. I have heard folks say, "But I'm afraid that was just me." Certainly that was you. You have the right to speak in tongues in Jesus' name. You do the talking just as much as you lay hands on the sick person. The Holy Ghost gives you the utterance; you do the talking. This is our right in the name of Jesus. It belongs to everyone, not just someone especially called. The ordinary child of God has just as much right to use the name of Jesus as anyone.

Let me call your attention to something else here. We do not have to struggle for faith. Some people think that if they just had enough faith, they could do these things. But notice that this passage of scripture does not say a word about faith. Jesus didn't say, "If they have enough faith . . ." He said, "These signs shall follow them that believe; In my name they shall . . ." and He went on to enumerate our rights through His name.

We do not have to struggle for faith. It is simply a matter of claiming our rights and boldly using what we know belongs to us.

The name of Jesus belongs to me as much as my hands and feet belong to me. When I awaken in the morning, I don't pray for God to give me faith to get up and walk. I just get up and walk because I know my feet are there and they are mine. Certainly the name of Jesus is just as much mine as my hands and feet are mine, and I can use His name.

Praying With Results

There are people who pray and pray, but the results do not prove that their prayers were of any value. If you do not get results when you pray, then you need to reexamine your methods. If you are not praying for results and expecting results, then there is no need to pray. Just as businesses expect to make a profit, so should we expect to profit when we pray. If a business was not getting results, if it was not making a profit, its management would immediately begin to re-evaluate its methods and make necessary changes. Industry demands the best technical education, it demands men trained to do their jobs. Christians too should make a business of prayer, the greatest business there is—God's business.

Prayer is of the utmost importance. The basis of Christianity from a practical side is a living religion that has touch with the living God who hears and answers prayer. Just simply talking into the air is not prayer. Taking up twenty minutes on Sunday morning giving God a homily on what His duties are toward the church is not prayer. Or giving the congregation a lecture over the shoulder of God is not prayer.

We should pray for results. If we pray and there are no results, it shows that we simply have the form without the power. All things that God has provided for us are offered to us through prayer, and if we do not have them it is because we have not made our prayer connection.

If you are praying without seeing any results, seek to find the trouble. Is God untrue? No, He's not untrue! Is the day of praying or of miracles over? No! Have we been depending upon the promises of a God who has gone bankrupt? No! Then there is something wrong somewhere, isn't there? Is it that we are not known in the bank of heaven?

Let us seek to find the cause, uproot any doubt and unbelief, pray as Jesus taught us to pray—to the Father in Jesus' name — for Jesus stands back of His Word. When we come according to God's Word, it cannot fail.

MEMORY TEXT:

"If ye shall ask any thing in my name, I will do it." *(John 14:14)*

THE LESSON IN ACTION: *"But be ye doers of the word, and not hearers only..."* James 1:22

This week I will put the lesson into practice by doing the following:

*There is tremendous power as two or more agree
in prayer concerning anything they may need.*

Lesson 5

The Prayer of Agreement

Matthew 18:18-20
Deuteronomy 32:30
Romans 8:26

Of all the many prayer promises in the Bible, perhaps none is more significant than the one in Matthew 18:19, the memory text quoted below. Yet many dedicated Christians go through life having a knowledge of the Word, having read and even studied this promise, without really appropriating it in their own lives. God didn't put all of these promises relative to prayer in the Bible just to fill up space. They are there for our benefit. They are there for us to use. They are there for us to act upon.

In order to get the full impact of what Jesus is saying in this verse of scripture, let us look at the verses preceding and following it.

MATTHEW 18:18-20

18 Verily I say unto you, Whatsoever ye shall bind on earth shall be bound in heaven: and whatsoever ye shall loose on earth shall be loosed in heaven.

19 Again I say unto you, That if two of you shall agree on earth as touching any thing that they shall ask, it shall be done for them of my Father which is in heaven.

20 For where two or three are gathered together in my name, there am I in the midst of them.

Notice the phrase in verse 19, "it shall be done for them of my Father which is in heaven." The strongest assertion one can make in the English language is to say "I shall" or "I will." We cannot make a stronger statement than that. In this scripture Jesus promised, *"It shall be done* for them of my Father which is in heaven." He also said, "If ye shall ask any thing in my name, I will do it" (John 14:14).

P.C. Nelson was a Greek scholar, and he did all of his personal Bible reading and private devotions from the Greek New Testament. He said that it was more beautiful than the English, and that there were a number of idioms that could not be translated in the English and still retain their fullest meaning. They had no English counterpart. Dr. Nelson said that the more literal rendering of Jesus' statement in the Greek is, "If you shall ask anything in my name, and I don't have it, then I will make it for you."

Authority to Loose and Bind

Looking at verse 20 of the above passage, "For where two or three are gathered together in my name, there am I in the midst of them," we usually apply this to a church service. Of course, it can refer to this, but what Jesus was really saying here is that wherever these two people are who agree, He is right there to make it good. Jesus was bringing out the fact that whatever we bind on earth shall be bound in heaven, and whatever we loose on earth shall be loosed in heaven. Heaven will back us up in what we do on earth. We have the authority to loose and to bind.

Instead of using this authority, however, too many folks just let the devil bind them. They think they can't help it if they are defeated and depressed. They

25

think there is nothing they can do about it. But they *can* do something about it by acting upon this scripture—by agreeing in prayer with just one other believer.

During 1957 our nation experienced an economic recession. Oregon was a state which felt the recession quite desperately. At the time I was preaching a revival campaign in Salem, Oregon. As I preached on the subject of the agreement prayer, a couple in the church decided to claim this promise and make it work for them. They had a lot which they had been trying to sell for two years with no success. Now that times were so difficult, it seemed impossible to sell it at all. Yet, they agreed in prayer that with the Lord's help they would be able to sell it.

When the man visited a real estate agent, he was told that since the agent hadn't been able to sell the lot when times were good, there was little hope that it would sell now. He did suggest that the man talk to a client who had previously been interested in the lot. The agent was not too optimistic, however, and said that if this client did not buy the lot, to come back and he would list it again and try once more to sell it.

Remembering Jesus' promise concerning agreement in prayer, the man approached the client with an offer to sell the lot again (at the same price they had discussed before). This time the man said he would take it.

For two years this couple had been in financial trouble, desperately needing to sell their lot. They could have had the money all the time if only they had exercised their authority by agreeing in prayer that "it shall be done for them of my Father which is in heaven." Instead of believing with the heart and saying it with the mouth, they had been praying that God would do something about it. They realized now that they should have done something about it. We have our

part to play. When we make our move, then God moves.

Multiplied Prayer Power

DEUTERONOMY 32:30

30 How should one chase a thousand, and two put ten thousand to flight, except their rock had sold them, and the Lord had shut them up?

We may be mighty in prayer alone, but we can be mightier with someone joining us. We read in the above verse that one can chase a thousand, but two can put ten thousand to flight. With someone agreeing with us in prayer, we can do ten times as much as we can do by ourselves. There doesn't have to be a great number. Just a husband and wife will do. Just two.

I was reading a book by Dr. George Truett, who for many years was pastor of the First Baptist Church in Dallas, Texas. One chapter of his book dealt with this subject of agreeing in prayer. He told of how as a young seminary student, he would go out during the summer and conduct revival meetings. While he was preaching in West Texas under a brush arbor, a big rancher about six feet, six inches tall in his cowboy boots came to him following the sermon one night and asked him if he believed the New Testament. Truett answered that he did. Then the rancher asked if he believed everything in it. Truett answered that he surely did. The rancher asked him if he believed Matthew 18:19. Truett said that he didn't know off hand what was in Matthew 18:19, but whatever it was he believed it, (We are all sure that we believe, but we have to act on it to get results.)

The rancher then quoted this verse of scripture to him and told him that he was the first preacher they had ever had who really believed it. He asked Truett to agree with him that his ranch foreman and family would be saved the next night. He promised to have them in church. Truett said that he would agree for their salvation. This big fellow then reached out and grabbed his hand and shook it. He said, "Lord, I finally found someone to agree with me. I've been looking for someone for years. This little preacher and I agree that John Compton and his family will be saved tomorrow night."

After a sleepless night of doing battle with the devil, Truett went to the meeting the next night and saw the rancher come in followed by the other man, his wife and three children. Truett preached a fiery evangelistic message and gave the invitation, but he couldn't seem to move the man toward the altar. Finally he told the Lord that he had done all he could do, that he was going to sing one more verse and then turn it over to Him.

On the next verse of the invitation hymn the oldest child, a girl of about thirteen, came forward. She knelt at the altar and then one of the other children followed. Finally all three children were praying at the altar. Then came the mother and finally the father.

At the conclusion of the service the rancher grabbed Truett again and said that he knew if only he could find someone to agree with him, it would work. Then he asked Truett to agree with him about his neighbor. At this point, Truett said, if that rancher had asked him to agree with him that the sun would rise in the West, he would have agreed. He was ready for anything. He said that he was young and didn't know any better then. He said that we get our heads educated at the expense of our hearts, but that simple folks just believe God's Word and receive results. For two weeks

> *According to Mark 9:23 all things are possible to a believing one and I am a believing one.*

the meeting continued. Every night the rancher asked Truett to agree with him for another family, and every night that family was saved. It works. God honors His promise regardless of who the person may be, regardless of denomination.

The Holy Spirit in the Ministry of Intercession

ROMANS 8:26

26 Likewise the Spirit also helpeth our infirmities: for we know not what we should pray for as we ought: but the Spirit itself maketh intercession for us with groanings which cannot be uttered.

The Greek translation of the last phrase of this verse reads, "with groanings that cannot be uttered in articulate speech." Therefore, this verse includes groanings and praying in tongues also. In connection with this Paul said, "For if I pray in an unknown tongue, my spirit prayeth, but my understanding is unfruitful" (I Cor. 14:14). The Amplified version of this verse reads, "My spirit, by the Holy Spirit within me, prayeth."

Notice in Romans 8:26 that we do not know what we should pray for. We cannot possibly know in our natural mind how to pray as we should, as there are so many things that are known only to God. But "the Spirit also helpeth our infirmities." The Holy Spirit will help us and will make intercession for us with groanings which cannot be uttered in articulate speech.

This does not mean that it is something the Holy Ghost does apart from you. That would make the Holy Ghost responsible for your prayer life, and He isn't. You are responsible for your prayer life. Notice that this verse says that He "helpeth." He is not sent to do your praying for you. He is sent to help you in every aspect of your life and especially your prayer life.

There are some things that come out

of your heart that cannot be expressed in words. It is the Holy Spirit helping you as these groanings come out of your spirit and escape your lips. It is the Holy Spirit in the ministry of intercession. A prayer of intercession is praying for another, not for yourself. An intercessor takes the place of another.

I do most of my praying in tongues. For instance, my son might have problems which I would know nothing about. I tell the Lord that I don't know how to pray for him as I ought, but I look to the Holy Spirit to give me utterance. Sometimes I pray for him an hour in tongues. Sometimes I may have a revelation or God will show me the answer just exactly. But whether there is a revelation or not, we can pray that way because we know it is Biblical. This kind of praying in the Spirit gets the job done when nothing else will. The Holy Spirit makes intercession through us to the throne of grace.

MEMORY TEXT:

"Again I say unto you, That if two of you shall agree on earth as touching any thing that they shall ask, it shall be done for them of my Father which is in heaven." *(Matt. 18:19)*

THE LESSON IN ACTION: *"But be ye doers of the word, and not hearers only . . ."* James 1:22

This week I will put the lesson into practice by doing the following:

Lesson 6

The Six Most Important Things in Prayer
(Part I)

John 16:23-24; Mark 11:24-26

Many times I have asked people, as they get up from praying, what they believe. Too often they have answered, "Well, I hope God heard me." I just tell them that He didn't. He said that "if you believe you shall receive," not "if you hope you shall receive." He didn't say to keep on keeping on until you get the answer. He said that when you pray you should believe that you receive.

When you believe that you receive, you don't have to pray all night long. You can go to bed and sleep peacefully, knowing that God has heard and will answer prayer. It's the most wonderful thing in the world to be able to pillow your head on the promises of God and go to sleep like a baby. Everything around you might be in turmoil, but right in the midst of it you can have peace.

Today's lesson deals with the six most important things the Christian should know about prayer.

Number 1: Pray to the Father in the Name of Jesus

JOHN 16:23-24

23 And in that day ye shall ask me nothing. Verily, verily, I say unto you, Whatsoever ye shall ask the Father in my name, he will give it you.

24 Hitherto have ye asked nothing in my name: ask, and ye shall receive, that your joy may be full.

When Jesus spoke the words quoted above He was here on earth. He was talking about the day in which we now live. He had not as yet gone to Calvary. He had not died and been buried. He had not risen from the dead. The New Testament covenant was not in force when He said this. His blood had not been carried into the Holy of Holies. His blood is the seal of the Covenant. Man had the promise of redemption, but had not yet received it. Eternal life had been promised but had not yet been provided. None had the new birth—they had only the promise of it. The new birth is available only under the New Covenant.

In the Old Covenant the New Covenant was prophesied. In the Old Covenant men's hearts were never changed. That is the reason they kept on sinning. They couldn't help but sin. Some of the greatest saints of the Old Testament sinned. Even after they were forgiven for one thing they would go and do something else. Their natures were all wrong. Their hearts were all wrong. They had only a covering for their sins.

But in the New Testament God said that He would take that old heart out of us and give us a new one. He said He would put a new spirit in us. This became available under the New Covenant,

> *According to John 14:6 Jesus is the only way to the Father. He is the way for salvation, for healing, for being made whole, for answers to prayer. We can come to the Father in the Name of Jesus.*

29

but it wasn't available while Jesus was on earth because the New Covenant wasn't in force then. He hadn't shed His blood yet. In this passage of scripture He was telling His disciples that after He goes to Calvary and is raised from the dead, the people are then to pray to His Father.

When it comes to prayer based on legal grounds, it should be addressed to the Father in the name of Jesus. We are not supposed to pray to Jesus. This is His instruction. Even what we refer to as the Lord's Prayer is not New Testament praying. While Jesus was here on earth the disciples asked Him to teach them to pray, and He taught them to pray, "Our Father . . ." This prayer didn't ask a thing in Jesus' name. His name wasn't even mentioned. This prayer was prayed under the Old Covenant. But under the New Covenant, which was sealed with the precious blood of Jesus, they were to pray to the Father in Jesus' name.

Let us focus our attention on the word, "whatsoever," in verse 23 of the above passage. So many times we say that we believe for an answer to prayer, "if it is God's will." But notice that this verse makes no such condition. It says, "Whatsoever ye shall ask the Father in my name, he will give it you." It must have been His will; otherwise He wouldn't have said it.

Why did Jesus say, "Whatsoever ye shall ask the Father in my name, he will give it you"? The answer is found in verse 24: ". . . that your joy may be full." Our joy certainly cannot be full if we are out of a job and our children are hungry. Our joy cannot be full if our body is racked with pain. Our joy cannot be full if there are problems in our home. Jesus said that the Father would give us "whatsoever" we ask in order that our "joy may be full." But there was a secret to success with this kind of praying. The

key is in the words, "Whatsoever ye shall *ask the Father in my name. . .*" We are to address our prayers to the Father in the name of Jesus.

Number 2: Believe That You Receive

MARK 11:24

24 Therefore I say unto you, What things soever ye desire, when ye pray, believe that ye receive them and ye shall have them.

Smith Wigglesworth once said that there is something about believing God that will cause Him to pass over a million people to get to you. God is a faith God and we are faith children of a faith God. He works on the principle of faith. We are saved by faith. "For by grace are ye saved through faith; and that not of yourselves: it is a gift of God: Not of works, lest any man should boast" (Eph. 2:8–9). We walk by faith and not by sight. It is the prayer of faith that God listens to.

He said that you can have the desires of your heart if you will believe that you receive them. You have to believe first, though. Most folks want to receive and then they will believe. But it is the other way around. The believing comes first.

I am convinced that if folks would quit praying about many of the things they pray about and begin thanking God for the answer, the answer would come right away. But they keep on in unbelief. If a person prays again, asking the same thing again, then he doesn't believe that he received the first time he asked. If he believed that he had received, he would be thanking God for it. Then it would be made manifest. The difference is that the faith Jesus was talking about in the verse quoted above is a heart faith, a spiritual faith, not a head faith. We get so used to walking by head faith. But we are to believe in our heart that we receive what we are praying for, even though we do not see the answer with our physical eyes.

This is true also of physical healing, but it seems more difficult to practice this faith for physical healing than for anything else because we have the body, with all its feelings and symptoms, with which we have to contend. Most people are going to believe that God has healed them when they can see the condition has grown better or when the symptoms are gone. They will believe that they are healed then. But anyone can believe what he can see. What Jesus was teaching us here is that we should believe when we pray and then we will receive.

For many years I have practiced this kind of faith, and this verse of scripture has been my standby. I have experienced this in my own life as I have prayed for the desires of my heart, believing that I receive them. Not only is it true for healing, but also in every other aspect of life. No matter what the need may be—material, spiritual or financial—this is the way that we receive.

Smith Wigglesworth said that with some people, if that for which they claim to be believing God doesn't come immediately, they are ready to give up. But, he says, this proves that they never believed God in the first place. Many times God permits our faith to be tried and tested right up to the end. But when you believe God you can stand firm though you are tested. I have been there and I know by experience. I learned many years ago just to laugh all the more when the going gets rough. I don't always feel like laughing, but I make myself laugh right in the face of the devil. I smile and say that I believe God.

When Paul was on board a ship headed for Rome, a great storm arose. All hope was gone that the ship and its passengers would be saved. In an attempt to save the ship, however, the crew threw all cargo overboard. But right in the midst of the storm's fury, Paul stood up and said that he believed God. You and I might not have to face a storm-tossed sea, but we do have to face storms in life. We too can stand, with the faith of Paul, and announce that we believe God.

Number 3: Forgive When You Pray

MARK 11:25–26

25 And when ye stand praying, forgive, if ye have ought against any: that your Father also which is in heaven may forgive you your trespasses.

26 But if ye do not forgive, neither will your Father which is in heaven forgive your trespasses.

Before we can expect an answer to our prayers, we must have a forgiving heart to any who may have wronged us. We cannot hold a grudge, we cannot keep an unforgiving spirit, if we want our prayers to reach God's throne of grace. Prayer will not work in an unforgiving heart.

No one can have an effective prayer life and have anything in his heart toward another. You cannot have revenge in your heart. You cannot have hatred in your heart. You cannot have that old "get-even" spirit in your heart. You are not responsible for that other person's life. You are responsible for your life. Another person's heart and what is in it cannot hinder you, but what you have in your heart against him can hinder you.

We must watch our inward man with all diligence. We cannot afford to allow a root of bitterness, a bit of envy, a spark of revenge to get in there. It will wreck our spiritual life. It will stall our prayer life. It will mar our faith and eventually shipwreck us.

A fellow once wanted me to pray that he would never have any more trouble with the devil. I told him that I didn't know anyone who was free from trouble with the devil, least of all me. We cannot pray that we won't have any more trouble with the devil, but we can learn to take authority over the devil. "Resist the devil, and he will flee from you" (James 4:7). We can learn to do something about the devil.

God prepares a table before us in the presence of our enemies. Right in the presence of the devil, Jesus is there. Right in the presence of the enemies of doubt and despair, we can sit at the table of victory and deliverance with Jesus. In the face of adverse circumstances we can believe that we receive.

⚔

MEMORY TEXT:

"Praying always with all prayer and supplication in the Spirit, and watching with all perseverance and supplication for all saints." *(Eph. 6:18)*

THE LESSON IN ACTION: *"But be ye doers of the word, and not hearers only..."* James 1:22

This week I will put the lesson into practice by doing the following:

When we allow the Holy Spirit to pray through us, to help us in our prayer life, we will see amazing answers to our prayers.

The Six Most Important Things in Prayer
(Part II)

Romans 8:26-27
I Corinthians 14:14-15
Jude 1:20; I Corinthians 14:4

EPHESIANS 6:18

18 Praying always with all prayer and supplication in the Spirit, and watching thereunto with all perseverance and supplication for all saints.

Moffat's translation of Ephesians 6:18, quoted above, says, "praying at all times with all manner of prayer." Another modern translation says, "praying with all kinds of prayer." The King James Version, even though it does not say "all kinds of prayer," says "praying always with all prayer," inferring that there is more than one kind of prayer. If there were not, it would merely have said, "praying always," and would have stopped there.

How desperately our nation needs prayer. How desperately the church needs prayer. How desperately we as individuals need prayer. Nothing can take the place of prayer for meeting the needs of our family.

In our last lesson we discussed three points in our study of the six most important things the Christian should know about prayer. They were: (1) Pray to the Father in the name of Jesus, (2) Believe that you receive, and (3) Forgive when

you pray. Today's lesson will cover the last three points in this topic.

Number 4: Depend Upon the Holy Spirit in Your Prayer Life

ROMANS 8:26-27

26 Likewise the Spirit also helpeth our infirmities: for we know not what we should pray for as we ought: but the Spirit itself maketh intercession for us with groanings which cannot be uttered.

27 And he that searcheth the hearts knoweth what is the mind of the Spirit, because he maketh intercession for the saints according to the will of God.

I CORINTHIANS 14:14-15

14 For if I pray in an unknown tongue, my spirit prayeth, but my understanding is unfruitful.

15 What is it then? I will pray with the spirit, and I will pray with the understanding also: I will sing with the spirit, and I will sing with the understanding also.

Christians everywhere pray with the understanding, but not all pray with the Spirit, as Paul speaks of in the verses quoted above. Many do not know that it is even possible to do so. Some in their haste and ignorance of the scriptures have said that tongues have been done away with. But if that be the case, how are we going to "pray with the spirit" today? Surely the Corinthian Christians didn't have a means of praying that we cannot have. We have the same means available to us today.

Paul said that when he prayed in an unknown tongue his spirit prayed. When you pray in tongues, it is your spirit praying by the Holy Spirit within you. You are groaning by the Holy Spirit within you groaning. I have sometimes been so burdened in prayer that I didn't have adequate words to express my feelings. All I could do was to groan from somewhere way down deep inside of me. Paul says that these groanings which escape our lips come from our spirit, from the innermost being. When this happens it is the Spirit helping us to pray, as we see in Romans 8:26.

The literal Greek translation of Romans 8:26 says, "The Spirit Himself maketh intercession for us with groanings that cannot be uttered in articulate speech." Articulate speech means your regular kind of speech. Speaking with tongues is not your regular kind of speech, so this verse includes speaking and praying with other tongues.

Paul said that the Holy Spirit would help us in our prayer life. Why? ". . . For we know not what we should pray for as we ought: but the Spirit itself maketh intercession for us . . ." (Verse 26). We do not always understand the entire situation surrounding the matter we are praying about. But the Holy Spirit does. And when we allow Him to pray through us, to help us in our prayer life, we will see amazing answers to our prayers.

If I know about things for which I ought to pray, then I can believe when I pray and I will receive them. However, there are things about which we should pray, but we do not know how to pray for them as we should. The Holy Spirit knows, however, and He can help us. It is easier to have faith for needs like paying the rent and buying groceries because we know what we are praying for. But there are some situations in life about which it is not quite so easy to pray.

Many have been the times in my own life when I have told the Lord that I didn't know exactly how I should pray concerning my own children. When I know there is a problem, I begin praying in tongues, and most of the time before I get through I have the answer to the problem.

Number 5: Pray the Prayer of Intercession

This point ties in closely with Number 4. Romans 8:26 says, ". . . The Spirit itself maketh intercession for us with groanings which cannot be uttered." The prayer of intercession is not for yourself. An intercessor is one who takes the place of another. You are interceding for another.

Every Spirit-filled believer can expect the Holy Spirit to help him in making intercession. This intercession can be in the area of the Spirit where it deals with salvation. It can deal with healing. It also includes praying for things about which we do not even know, but the Holy Spirit has knowledge of them.

After a time of praying in the Spirit we will know whether we are praying in tongues as a means of building ourselves up spiritually and worshiping God, as we will discuss in point number 6, or whether it is intercessory prayer.

On occasion and sometimes over a period of time I have had a burden of intercession before I even know for whom I am praying. I can tell when I am in intercession or travail for someone who is lost. If you are taking the place of a lost one, you will have that same lost feeling in your own spirit. And as we pray in the Spirit, interceding for that one, the Holy Spirit will deal with his heart and bring him under conviction of sin.

Number 6: Edify Yourself by Praying in the Holy Spirit

JUDE 1:20

20 But ye, beloved, building up yourselves on your most holy faith praying in the Holy Ghost.

I CORINTHIANS 14:4

4 He that speaketh in an unknown tongue edifieth himself . . .

There is one phase of speaking with tongues in our prayer life that is not praying for someone else, it is not interceding for anyone else. It is purely a means of personal spiritual edification. It aids us spiritually and edifies us. We all need this kind of praying. We cannot help others, we cannot edify others unless we ourselves have been edified.

Praying in this manner has a three-fold value. First, it is a means of spiritual edification. It affects us individually. Secondly, it is a means of praying for things about which we do not know. Thirdly, the Holy Spirit helps us make intercession.

Speaking in tongues is not only an initial evidence of the Holy Spirit's indwelling, but it is a continual experience for the rest of one's life. It is to assist in the worship of God. It is a flowing stream that should never dry up. It will enrich your life spiritually.

We will continue in our study of praying in tongues in our next lesson.

MEMORY TEXT:

"Praying always with all prayer and supplication in the Spirit, and watching thereunto with all perseverance and supplication for all saints."

(Eph. 6:18)

THE LESSON IN ACTION: *"But be ye doers of the word, and not hearers only..."* James 1:22

This week I will put the lesson into practice by doing the following:

Every believer can interpret his prayers in the Spirit, thus gaining spiritual understanding of them.

Lesson 8

Interpreting Our Prayers in the Spirit

I Corinthians 14:13-17; 27-28

Praying in the Spirit is not something which belongs only to the minister. It belongs to every believer. It is for every single one of us. Much has been accomplished through those who have yielded their prayer lives to the manifestation of the Holy Spirit through them, but how much greater results we would see if there were more Christians praying in the Spirit.

I CORINTHIANS 14:13-17

13 Wherefore let him that speaketh in an unknown tongue pray that he may interpret.

14 For if I pray in an unknown tongue, my spirit prayeth, but my understanding is unfruitful.

15 What is it then? I will pray with the spirit, and I will pray with the understanding also: I will sing with the spirit, and I will sing with the understanding also.

16 Else when thou shalt bless with the spirit, how shall he that occupieth the room of the unlearned say Amen at thy giving of thanks, seeing he understandeth not what thou sayest?

17 For thou verily givest thanks well, but the other is not edified.

God, speaking through the apostle Paul, said, "Wherefore let him that speaketh in an unknown tongue pray that he may interpret" (Verse 13). God certainly is not going to tell us to pray for something that we cannot have. I am convinced that every believer should be able to pray and interpret his own prayers, even though he may never interpret a message in tongues publicly. It is my observation that one can interpret without being an interpreter. We will explain this point more fully later in the lesson.

Everyone who speaks in tongues could pray that he interpret (and God tells us to). What point would there be in His telling us to pray for something we could not have? Would the Spirit of God tell us through the Apostle Paul to pray for something that we couldn't have? That would of course be utter folly. The fact that He has told us to pray that we may interpret means that He has made this available to every believer.

Every believer should be able to pray in tongues, praying in the Spirit, because we are encouraged to do so. In praying in the Spirit we should pray that we could also interpret. Notice why God wants us to do this. In I Corinthians 14:13 we read, "Wherefore let him that speaketh in an unknown tongue pray that he may interpret." Then the next two verses which follow begin with the conjunction *for*. A conjunction is a connecting word. Therefore, Paul was going on with what he had said in the previous verse when he said, *"For* if I pray in an unknown tongue, my spirit prayeth, but my understanding is unfruitful." If we could interpret our prayer, our understanding would no longer be unfruitful. It would then be fruitful. It would be helpful many times to know what you are praying about when you are praying in the Spirit. There are some things about

36

which we pray that we need to know the interpretation. We need to know because it would help us if our mind were enlightened.

However, I would never interpret those prayers whereby one edifies and builds himself up. These are merely prayers of worship and praise and such prayers need not be interpreted.

Praying With the Spirit and With the Understanding

Verse 15 continues right along and says, "What is it then? I will pray with the spirit, and I will pray with the understanding also . . ." There is a further meaning to this verse than that which we have generally accepted. It means that we can pray both ways—with the spirit and with the understanding—but it also means that if I will pray that I may interpret, then I can pray in the spirit and pray to interpret it. Then I will have understanding of what I have prayed about and can pray with the understanding also.

I have prayed in this manner since 1938 when I was baptized with the Holy Ghost. In those days we didn't have any teaching along these lines. Some even thought that if a person was filled with the Holy Spirit and spoke in tongues, it was not necessary for him to speak in tongues ever again. (Sadly, many Christians still do not rise above this level today.) When I would speak in tongues while praying after I was first filled with the Holy Spirit, I would stop because I wasn't sure if it was right or not. About a year later as I studied the Word I saw that it was right, that this blessing was for us today.

I interpreted my prayers long before I did any interpreting in public. I know from experience the difference it makes in one's prayer life.

Some of my first experiences along this line came as I was seeking God and waiting on Him as a new believer deeply in love with the Lord. I would be praying about my services and the messages I was to preach when the Spirit would move upon me in this fashion. As a young single man of 21, I was so wrapped up in spiritual things that I didn't have time for girls and dating. In fact, I seldom thought about girls. And the farthest thing from my mind was the thought of marriage. One day while praying in the Spirit I began to interpret my prayer. I found out that I was praying about the girl I was to marry. I also learned that we would have two children, the oldest a boy and the second one a girl. I was not prophesying, I was interpreting my prayer in tongues. I would pray in tongues a few words, then pray the interpretation.

Everything came to pass just as the interpretation said it would. That same year I got married. Then when we were expecting our first child, I knew it would be a boy. In fact, we didn't pick out any other name except a boy's name. When we were expecting our second child, I knew it would be a girl and again we picked out only a girl's name. Some of our relatives were skeptical and asked, "What if it isn't a girl?" I said, "I'm not going by 'what if's.' " When the baby was born, it was a lovely daughter.

Tongues and Interpretation— For Public or Private Use?

As mentioned earlier, the fact that one may interpret does not mean that he is an interpreter. The two are related but are not the same thing. To illustrate, an automobile, a truck and a bus are totally different vehicles, yet they are all in the same family. Just because a person owns

The Father loves me as He loves Jesus according to John 17:23.

a car and can drive it does not mean that he is a trucker. Even if he owned a truck, that would not necessarily mean that he could drive it. And because a man is a bus driver does not mean that he is a trucker. They are all different yet related. The same is true of tongues and interpretation.

I Corinthians 14:27-28

27 If any man speak in an unknown tongue, let it be by two, or at the most by three, and that by course; and let one interpret.

28 But if there be no interpreter, let him keep silence in the church; and let him speak to himself, and to God.

In verse 28 we read, "But if there be no interpreter . . ." or in other words if no interpreter is present, inferring that there are those who are *interpreters*.

We make a great mistake by thinking that tongues and interpretation is just for public use. There is a public side to it under certain circumstances, but as we see from the passage of scripture above, its main use is private.

As I said, I interpreted my own prayers long before I interpreted publicly. When I began to interpret my prayers in private, it was like driving that car. When I began to interpret publicly, it was like driving that truck. It was partly the same, but it was different. One stands in a different office, on a different plane, in a different area. When I first interpreted my prayers that was all I could interpret. I could not interpret anyone else's prayers. I did not interpret a message in tongues. Later, however, I received the gift of interpretation.

Notice that the scripture does not say, "Let him that speaketh in an unknown tongue pray that he may have the gift of interpretation." It says, "Let him . . .

pray that he may interpret." Interpret what? Interpret his prayer. Why? In order that he can "pray with the spirit, and . . . with the understanding also." This would not make him an interpreter, it would make him one who prays in the spirit.

When I received the gift of interpretation and became an interpreter I still couldn't interpret what people prayed. But I could interpret all public utterances, and I still can although I don't always do it.

I have learned by experience that when someone speaks in tongues I can interpret if I respond to the Spirit. In the passage of scripture in I Corinthians 14:27-28, Paul infers that an interpreter can. He said, "If there be no interpreter . . ." inferring that some are interpreters, having the gift of interpretation, while others do not. An interpreter might not be present when others are. And if no interpreter is present, then the one giving the message should be silent. This implies that an interpreter could always interpret the messages.

I do not always interpret all the prayers I pray in tongues. Only as the Lord wills and as it is necessary do I interpret these prayers. In Romans 8:26 we read, "Likewise the Spirit also helpeth our infirmities: for we know not what we should pray for as we ought: but the Spirit itself maketh intercession for us with groanings which cannot be uttered." If you don't know what to pray for as you ought, you can pray in the Spirit and then interpret. Then you will know what you prayed for. Then you will be praying "with the spirit, and . . . with the understanding also."

I am convinced that every believer should be praying in the Spirit and with

I have a Good Shepherd; I do not want according to John 10:14 and Psalm 23:1.

the understanding—not just a prayer out of his understanding, but praying the interpretation so that he can understand his prayers in the Spirit. ⛨

THE LESSON IN ACTION: *"But be ye doers of the word, and not hearers only..."* James 1:22

This week I will put the lesson into practice by doing the following:

Lesson 9

Tongues— A Flowing Stream of Praise

I Corinthians 12:7-11
Ephesians 5:18-19; John 7:37-39

Having studied in the last two lessons the necessity and value of praying in tongues, let us now take a closer look at this manifestation itself—the different kinds of tongues and their different uses.

Tongues—One of the Nine Gifts of the Spirit

I Corinthians 12:7–11

7 But the manifestation of the Spirit is given to every man to profit withal.

8 For to one is given by the Spirit the word of wisdom; to another the word of knowledge by the same Spirit;

9 To another faith by the same Spirit; to another the gifts of healing by the same Spirit;

10 To another the working of miracles; to another prophecy; to another discerning of spirits; to another divers kinds of tongues; to another the interpretation of tongues:

11 But all these worketh that one and the selfsame Spirit, dividing to every man severally as he will.

In the verses above are listed the nine gifts, or nine manifestations of the Spirit —nine ways in which the Holy Spirit manifests Himself. Three of these gifts are gifts of inspiration or utterance. These vocal gifts are designed as an inspiration in public worship. Of these, the gift of tongues is the most prominent.

Tongues with interpretation is distinctive with this dispensation. All of the other gifts of the Spirit were manifested in the Old Testament. Even in the life and ministry of Jesus all the other gifts of the Spirit were manifested, except tongues and interpretation. Since tongues and interpretation are distinctive with this dispensation, they would naturally be distributed and used more frequently in the church than the other gifts. This is the reason that we have an abundance of this manifestation.

Divers kinds of tongues are supernatural utterances given by the Holy Ghost. These are languages never learned by the speaker nor understood by him. Usually they are not understood by the hearers. There are exceptions to this, however, as there have been times when the words someone speaks in tongues have been understood by someone present.

A minister told me of an experience he had while preaching at a mission station in Mexico. He said, "I preached for about five nights with the local missionary interpreting my sermon in Spanish. One night I saw one of the most beautiful sights I have ever seen in my life. A rather large and homely Mexican woman came forward to receive the Holy Ghost after I had preached. The power of God fell on her and she began to speak in the most perfect English I had ever heard. I could understand everything she said. She had never been to school a day in her life and her native tongue was Spanish. Hearing her speak in my language— English — a language she had never learned, really did something for me. I have never been the same since."

Another instance in which tongues were understood by a listener but not by the speaker involved a woman missionary to India. While home on furlough she attended a service at a Bible institute. One of the students gave a message in tongues, but no interpretation came. As everyone waited and wondered why there was no interpretation, she stood and said, "That student was speaking one of the dialects of India. I understood every word that was said. This was for me and that is the reason no interpretation was given. Through this message God spoke to me telling me that He wanted me to go back and what He wanted me to do."

Tongues—The Initial Evidence of the Baptism of the Holy Spirit

Speaking in tongues is always manifested when people are baptized in the Holy Spirit. "And they were all filled with the Holy Ghost, and began to speak with other tongues, as the Spirit gave them utterance" (Acts 2:4). I do not argue with those who claim to have the Holy Spirit even though they have never spoken in tongues. After all, the Holy Spirit does a work of regeneration when a person is born again, and the Bible tells us that "The Spirit itself beareth witness with our spirit, that we are the children of God" (Rom. 8:16).

Many years ago as a young pastor hungry for the deeper things of God, reading the New Testament I came to the conclusion that if I received the same Holy Ghost that the disciples did on the day of Pentecost, I wanted the same accompanying sign. If I didn't have the same sign—speaking in tongues—then I had no scriptural evidence that I was filled with the same Holy Ghost with which they were filled. Thank God, I did receive that same Holy Ghost and did

speak with tongues as the Spirit gave utterance.

Smith Wigglesworth was one to argue that he was already filled and baptized with the Holy Ghost even though at that time he had not spoken in other tongues. When he heard that some folks in an Episcopal church were speaking in tongues he went to see about it. He found that the pastor and his wife had received the baptism in the Holy Ghost as well as many of their members. They asked him, "Do you have the Holy Ghost?" Wigglesworth replied that he did. "Well, have you spoken with tongues?" they asked.

"No, but I'm just as much filled with the Holy Ghost as you are," he answered.

After awhile, however, he began to see the necessity of speaking in tongues and went to the Episcopal rectory to ask the pastor to pray for him, but he wasn't there.

The pastor's wife said, "I'll pray for you."

Smith said, "Lay your hands on my head and pray that I'll get the tongues."

"You don't want the tongues," she said, "you want the Holy Ghost. The tongues will take care of itself."

He argued, "But I already have the Holy Ghost."

"Never mind, just kneel down there," the pastor's wife said. She was tired of arguing with him. Wigglesworth knelt and as hands were laid upon him, the power of God came over him and he began to speak in other tongues. He later said, "The Holy Ghost settled all my arguments for me. I had been arguing and discussing the subject with them every day that I had the Holy Ghost just as much as they did. In a moment's time I saw that I had never really been filled with the Holy Ghost until then. I had had some wonderful experiences as a minister as God had blessed me and anointed me to preach. We had seen

41

many saved and even healed. But I had never really been filled with the Holy Ghost until then. When you get an experience inside the Word of God, you have an experience outside the realm of argument. Before I had only an argument, but now I have an experience with God."

There is a difference in purpose and use of ministering tongues in public assembly and speaking with tongues as a Spirit-baptized individual. On the other hand, the essence of tongues is the same and the source of the tongues is the same. It comes from the Holy Ghost. If people are being filled with the Holy Ghost in our midst, then we are going to have people speaking in tongues.

Tongues in the Believer's Prayer Life

Too, the Spirit-baptized believer does not have to stop speaking in tongues after his initial experience. He can continue to use tongues in his prayer and worship to God even though he may not be used to minister in tongues in public.

Howard Carter, founder of the oldest Pentecostal Bible school in the world, said, "We must not forget that the speaking with other tongues is not only an initial evidence or sign of the Holy Spirit's indwelling, but it is a continual experience for the rest of one's life to assist in the worship of God. Speaking with tongues is a flowing stream that should never die out, but will enrich the life spiritually."

Sometimes we become satisfied, we feel that we have arrived spiritually, so to speak, because we have been baptized in the Holy Ghost and spoken in tongues for awhile. A pastor once told me about a young man in his church who had been seeking the baptism of the Holy Ghost. The man came every night to their revival services, and finally one night he

> According to I John 1:9 when I sin if I confess, "I have sinned. I have failed God. Forgive me Lord, in Jesus' name." Then the Lord does two things. He forgives me and He cleanses me.

received. After that he stopped coming to the services. When the pastor asked him about it he said, "Why, I finally got through." But we don't get through. That is just the beginning.

EPHESIANS 5:18-19

18 And be not drunk with wine, wherein is excess; but be filled with the Spirit;

19 Speaking to yourselves in psalms and hymns and spiritual songs, singing and making melody in your heart to the Lord.

Paul wrote the above verses to the born-again, Spirit-filled believers in the church at Ephesus. He told them to "be filled with the Spirit." He told them to be drunk on the Spirit and not wine. The Greek says, "be being filled"; in other words, maintain a constant experience. Keep drinking.

Then Paul gave them the characteristic of the Spirit-filled life. "Speaking to yourselves in psalms and hymns and spiritual songs, singing and making melody in your heart to the Lord" (Verse 19). A psalm is a spiritual poem or an ode. It may rhyme or it may not rhyme, but there is an element of poetry about it. It is given by the inspiration of the Holy Spirit on the spur of the moment. It can come by tongues and interpretation or by prophecy.

JOHN 7:37-39

37 In the last day, that great day of the feast, Jesus stood and cried, saying, If any man thirst, let him come unto me, and drink.

38 He that believeth on me, as the scripture hath said, out of his belly shall flow rivers of living water.

39 (But this spake he of the Spirit, which they that believe on him should receive: for the Holy Ghost was not yet given; because that Jesus was not yet glorified.)

Water is a type of the Holy Spirit. Jesus stood at the last day of the feast and said to drink of the Spirit. He was encouraging the people to stay filled with the Spirit. By so doing, we can overcome the devil and the sins of this world, and can live a life that is pleasing to Christ. ". . . Walk in the Spirit, and ye shall not fulfil the lust of the flesh" (Gal. 5:16).

MEMORY TEXT:

"And be not drunk with wine, wherein is excess; but be filled with the Spirit." *(Eph. 5:18)*

THE LESSON IN ACTION: *"But be ye doers of the word, and not hearers only..."* James 1:22

This week I will put the lesson into practice by doing the following:

As we pray in the Spirit, our spirit is not bound by human limitations.

Lesson 10

Prayer on a New Dimension

I Corinthians 14:2, 4, 18

Some people ask, "What is the use of speaking with tongues?" There are also those who have been filled with the Holy Spirit and have spoken with tongues but see no reason to continue to speak in tongues in their daily prayer life.

Evidently God thought that speaking in tongues was very important, for He inspired the apostle Paul to devote an entire chapter in the Bible—I Corinthians 14—to this subject. Although all will agree on the utmost importance of prayer, where in the Bible can we find an entire chapter on prayer? The paying of tithes and offerings is also very important. We could not carry on the work of God without them. But where in the Word of God do we see a whole chapter given to the subject? Water baptism is also important. But again we do not find an entire chapter devoted to the subject.

What I am trying to say is that God does not put unnecessary things in His Word. He has not filled the Bible with unimportant statements. The teachings on the subject of speaking in tongues are vital and necessary to every successful Christian.

Speaking Secrets to God

I CORINTHIANS 14:2, 4, 18

2 For he that speaketh in an unknown tongue speaketh not unto men, but unto God: for no man understandeth him; howbeit in the spirit he speaketh mysteries.

4 He that speaketh in an unknown tongue edifieth himself...

18 I thank my God, I speak with tongues more than ye all...

In verse 2 above when Paul said, "For he that speaketh in an unknown tongue speaketh not unto men, but unto God," he was not talking at this time about ministering tongues in public assembly. He was talking about the individual Spirit-filled believer talking in tongues in his private prayer life. This also includes praying in tongues during prayer services at the altar in church because we come here to talk to God.

Paul continued, in verse 2, "... howbeit in the spirit he speaketh mysteries." Weymouth's translation of this verse says, "in the Spirit he speaks divine secrets." God has devised a way whereby we may speak to Him supernaturally. "Howbeit in the Spirit he speaks divine secrets." He talks secrets with God.

While I was holding a meeting in Mesa, Arizona, the pastor there told me the story of a young Jewish boy who attended his church. It seemed that he didn't have too many friends so one of the boys in the church befriended him. He invited the Jewish boy to come to church with him. At first the Jewish boy refused, saying that he didn't believe in Christ. However, he got to thinking that he shouldn't be so obstinate for, after all, this boy was the only one who had been kind to him. So he agreed to go with him.

During the service a woman stood and gave a message in tongues. No interpretation was given however. The pastor told me, "I waited for a few minutes, but finally when there was no interpretation to the message in tongues, we went on with the service. As I was shaking hands with the people at the conclusion of the service, the Jewish boy asked me, "Who was that lady who was talking to me?"

"At first I didn't understand what he meant. He went on to explain, 'That lady who got up in the service and talked to me. She spoke my language and even called my name. She told me what I had been thinking. She told me that Christ was the Messiah and that I should believe on Him.' He seemed to resent her talking directly to him in front of the crowd.

"I said to the boy, 'That dear lady is a widow who has only about a fifth-grade education. She takes in washings for a living. She speaks no languages other than English.' Then I called the lady over and introduced her to him so that he could see for himself that she was a very uneducated woman. The following Sunday night the Jewish boy was back in our services again, and that night he gave his heart to Christ."

This young Jewish boy received Christ as the Messiah and his Saviour as a result of a humble little widow who yielded to the Spirit's operation through her to speak to a lost boy.

Spiritual Edification

Verse 4 of I Corinthians 14 says, "He that speaketh in an unknown tongue edifieth himself..." This means that he builds himself up spiritually. Jude 20 says, "But ye, beloved, building up yourselves on your most holy faith, praying in the Holy Ghost." This does not say that praying in the Holy Ghost will give you faith, it says that it builds you up "on your most holy faith." It is a means of spiritual edification.

While I was pastor of a community church the lady in whose home I stayed was desperately ill with an ulcerated stomach and could eat nothing but baby food and a few raw eggs mixed in milk. She even had trouble keeping that on her stomach.

One day she received the baptism of the Holy Ghost. I was not present at the time, but she told me of her experience of being filled with the Spirit and speaking in other tongues. No one laid hands on her to pray for her healing, but from the moment that she received the Holy Ghost she was instantly healed and could eat anything she wanted.

Surely no one could find fault with an experience that can bring both healing and blessing. This woman was a believer, a wonderful child of God, and a dedicated Christian. By praying in tongues she built herself up on her most holy faith and her faith began to operate.

I have seen this happen many times. I have seen people with incurable conditions receive the baptism of the Holy Ghost, speak with tongues, and become healed instantly. Some of these same people were ones we had prayed for with the laying on of hands, but had failed to receive their healing.

We know that speaking with tongues is a real spiritual boost to a person. It edifies him and builds him up.

New Dimensions in Praise

Speaking with tongues is a way that we can magnify God. We read in Acts 10:46 concerning Cornelius and his household, "For they heard them speak with tongues, and magnify God...."

I was a young minister for several years before receiving the Baptism of the Holy Spirit. I had some wonderful times in prayer. God loves His children, no matter who they are, or how deeply they may have gone into the things of the Spirit. But many times I went away from my place of prayer disappointed even though I was blessed. I felt as if something was missing.

45

I would try to tell God how much I loved Him. I would use all the descriptive adjectives I had at my disposal to tell God how wonderful He is. I would exhaust my vocabulary. Yet in my spirit I felt that I had not said what I wanted to say. This was because my spirit wanted to pray, too, apart from my understanding. "For if I pray in an unknown tongue, my spirit prayeth, but my understanding is unfruitful" (I Cor. 14:14).

Since I have received the Holy Spirit and now pray in tongues, all this has changed. I can communicate with God on a new dimension. My spirit need not be bound by earthly vocabularies. It can soar beyond the limitations of human speech. My spirit is enabled by the indwelling Holy Spirit to say what it wants to say.

I cannot begin to estimate the worth of praying in the Spirit in my life. As I have traveled on the evangelistic field for many years, having to spend much time away from home, again and again the Holy Spirit has alerted me to needs in my family. I have been awakened in the night by the Spirit's urging to pray concerning a problem that has arisen at home. Immediately I go to prayer saying, "I don't know what is wrong. I don't

know the source of the trouble, but You know everything." I ask the Holy Spirit within me, who is my Helper, to help me pray about this situation, whatever it might be, in the way it should be prayed about. Then I begin praying in tongues. I have prayed as much as six hours in tongues. Many times He has let me know what I am praying about and the answer to it. Whether He does or not, I know it is right, and in a few days I see how it works out.

Praying in the Spirit has been such a blessing to my life that I want to encourage Christians everywhere to make this a part of their prayer life too. I want you to know the joy of fellowshiping with the Lord in the Spirit. I want you to allow the Holy Spirit to help you with praying. I want to invite you to come on in and communicate with God supernaturally. God wants to do so much more for you. He wants to communicate with you in a better way. †

MEMORY TEXT:

"For if I pray in an unknown tongue, my spirit prayeth . . ."
(I Cor. 14:14)

THE LESSON IN ACTION: *"But be ye doers of the word, and not hearers only . . ."* James 1:22

This week I will put the lesson into practice by doing the following:

Lesson 11

Kinds of Prayer

Matthew 21:22
Mark 11:24; Luke 22:42

Moffat's translation of Ephesians 6:18, quoted above, reads, "Praying with all manner of prayer . . ." Another translation says, "Praying with all kinds of prayer . . ." In today's lesson we will look at some of the different kinds of prayer in the New Testament.

Just as there are numerous different games which come under the general classification of sports, so there are many different kinds of prayer that we often lump together under one general category of prayer. We need to realize that as certain rules govern certain games in the area of sports, so there are certain principles or rules, spiritual laws so to speak, that govern certain kinds of praying. The ones that might apply to one type of prayer would not necessarily apply to another type of prayer. In sports the rules which apply to baseball would not apply to football. If one tried to use the same rules for both games, he would get terribly confused.

A visitor from Europe was taken by his host to see a baseball game in New York City. He didn't know much about the game as it is not played in his country. He couldn't understand the various expressions used and asked a number of questions. We are this way sometimes spiritually. Thus, though there are all kinds of prayer, the same rules don't apply in each case. If you try to apply them, you will become very confused.

The Prayer of Petition

MATTHEW 21:22

22 And all things, whatsoever ye shall ask in prayer, believing, ye shall receive.

MARK 11:24

24 Therefore I say unto you, What things soever ye desire, when ye pray, believe that ye receive them, and ye shall have them.

By far the most frequent prayer of most Christians is the prayer of petition. We are always petitioning, or asking, God to do something for us. This is scriptural, of course, for He has told us to "ask in prayer, believing . . ."

The prayer of petition must be a prayer of faith. This is primarily an individual situation. It concerns your desires. It concerns your needs and problems. It is your praying, not someone else praying with you or for you. It is not someone else agreeing with you in prayer. When you pray, you believe that you receive, and if you will do that, you will have it. He is concerned about our needs and wants to meet them for us.

In the Old Testament God promised His people more than just spiritual blessings. He promised them that they would prosper financially and materially. He told them that He would take sickness away from their midst and would give them long life. ". . . The number of thy days I will fulfill" (Exod. 23:26). He told them that if they would keep His commandments, they would eat the good of the land.

God is just as interested in His people today as He was then. He is concerned about everything that touches our lives. He has made provision for us. "Beloved,

47

I wish above all things that thou mayest prosper and be in health, even as thy soul prospereth" (III John 1:2).

Jesus said, "If ye then, being evil, know how to give good gifts unto your children, how much more shall your Father which is in heaven give good things to them that ask him?" (Matt. 7:11). We must realize that it is God's will that our needs—spiritual, physical and material—be met.

> Jesus is at the right hand of the Father, the place of authority, and we are seated with Him. We have died with Him and have been raised with Him. This is *according to Ephesians 1:20; 2:5,6.*

Some people think that they should conclude every prayer with the words, "If it be thy will." They claim that this was the way Jesus prayed. However, Jesus prayed this way on only one occasion. When He stood at Lazarus' tomb, He didn't say, ". . . if it be thy will . . ." He said, "I thank you because you hear me always," then He commanded Lazarus to come forth.

This prayer was to change something. Anytime we are praying to do something or change something, we need not put an "if" in our prayer. If we do, we are using the wrong rule and it won't work. We need to claim God's promise for our petition and *"believe* that ye receive them."

What kind of prayer was it that Jesus put an "if" in?

The Prayer of Consecration

LUKE 22:42

42 Saying, Father, if thou be willing, remove this cup from me: nevertheless not my will, but thine, be done.

In the Garden of Gethsemane Christ prayed the prayer of submission, of consecration and dedication, ". . . if thou be willing . . . nevertheless not my will . . ." He wanted to do what the Father wanted Him to do. It was not a prayer of petition. It was not a prayer to get something or to change something. It was a prayer of consecration.

When we consecrate our lives for God's use, to go anywhere and do anything He wants us to do, we pray this kind of prayer. In a prayer of consecration and dedication we pray, "if it be thy will."

When it comes to changing things or getting something from God, however, we do not pray, "if it be thy will," for we already have God's Word concerning it. We know it is His will that our needs be met.

MEMORY TEXT:

"Praying always with all prayer and supplication in the Spirit, and watching there unto with all perseverance and supplication for all saints."
(Eph. 6:18)

THE LESSON IN ACTION: *"But be ye doers of the word, and not hearers only..."* James 1:22

This week I will put the lesson into practice by doing the following:

Lesson 12

The Prayer
of Worship
(Part I)

Acts 13:1-4

As we mentioned in the last lesson, most of our prayers are the petition type of prayer. Too many of us are like the little boy who prayed, "Lord, my name is Jimmy, and I'll take everything you'll give me." This seems to be the only kind of prayer we know anything about. If that is all we are doing, I wonder if sometimes the Lord doesn't get a bit tired of it—just "give me." We need to take time to wait on God and to minister to the Lord—time when we are not asking Him for anything, when we are not petitioning, but are ministering to Him.

Not only do we need this as individuals in our private prayer lives, but we also need this kind of prayer service as a group. We read of a group in the New Testament church who had such a service.

ACTS 13:1-4

1 Now there were in the church that was at Antioch certain prophets and teachers; as Barnabas, and Simeon that was called Niger, and Lucius of Cyrene, and Manaen, which had been brought up with Herod the tetrarch, and Saul.

2 As they ministered to the Lord, and fasted, the Holy Ghost said, Separate me Barnabas and Saul for the work whereunto I have called them.

3 And when they had fasted and prayed, and laid their hands on them, they sent them away.

4 So they, being sent forth by the Holy Ghost, departed unto Seleucia; and from thence they sailed to Cyprus.

Today when Christians gather for a church service, we mostly minister to one another. Our services are designed that way. We sing songs, but in very few of them do we minister to the Lord; we minister to one another. We sing special solo numbers, but still we are not ministering to the Lord; we are ministering to one another. When we pray in church, our praying is primarily a petition. We are petitioning the Lord to move in our midst, to manifest Himself among us, and to meet our individual needs. Then when the minister stands to speak, he is not ministering to the Lord, he is ministering to the congregation. When the service is over, if we do have a time of waiting on God in prayer, this usually consists of petitioning prayer again. We come not necessarily to minister to the Lord, but to pray and seek God on our own behalf.

However, the Christians we read about in the account above in Acts 13:1-4 came together and "ministered to the Lord, and fasted . . ." (Verse 2). More than one person was involved in this account, for it says, "As *they* ministered to the Lord, and fasted . . ." This is the true prayer of worship.

God's Desire for Man's Praise

God made man so He would have someone with whom to have fellowship. He made man for His own pleasure. It is true that God is concerned about us and wants to meet our every need. But even more than that He wants our love, our worship and fellowship with Him.

49

He is our Father for we are born of God. No earthly parent ever enjoyed the fellowship of his children more than God enjoys the fellowship of His sons and daughters.

In one revival meeting we held I decided to do something a little different. After about six weeks of meetings I announced to the congregation one night, "Let's have some different kinds of services. For three nights out of these remaining two weeks I want us to come together to minister to the Lord. I may read from the Word just a little bit and make a few comments, but I am not going to do any preaching. We are not going to come to petition God to do anything. We are coming as a group to wait on the Lord, to minister to the Lord and worship Him. If you don't want to pray in this way, do not come on these particular nights.

"I don't want us to come and wait for just ten minutes. I want us to come with the thought in mind that we will wait at least an hour in prayer, perhaps longer. We will minister to the Lord, praise Him and tell Him how much we love Him, and thank Him for His goodness and mercy."

One might expect the crowd to have fallen off on those nights. It didn't. Just as many people came out and praised the Lord. I found that they wanted to wait on God. And in that kind of an atmosphere, God did minister to us in unusual ways. Although that was many years ago, I still see results today of things the Lord said to me which convince me that we miss out on many blessings because we don't take time to get into the right attitude of worship and to minister to the Lord.

The Power of Praise

Let me call your attention to the fact that this is the kind of atmosphere in

God has told me He has blotted out my transgressions and then does not remember what they were in *Isaiah 43:25.*

which God can move. "As they ministered to the Lord, and fasted, *the Holy Ghost said . . .*" With hearts yielded to the Lord, full of love and praise, the Holy Spirit can manifest Himself and make known God's will and leading for the lives of His children.

A minister told me of an experience he had once which illustrates the power of praise. Once very early in his ministry, while he was a young evangelist, he was staying at the pastor's home during one of his revival meetings. During the night a call came for the pastor to come pray for a baby who was having convulsions. The pastor had been called out of town to preach a funeral, but the pastor's wife asked this young evangelist to go with her and a few other faithful Christians to pray for the sick child.

Relating the experience to me, he said, "We rebuked the devil, we prayed at the top of our voices and went through all the motions that we sometimes feel are necessary in order to get God to hear our prayers. After about forty minutes of such rigorous praying, the child was no better but continued having convulsions.

"I had done about all I knew to do. I'd done everything I'd seen anybody else do. But nothing happened. Then as I got quiet, it seemed that the group who were gathered there to pray also grew quiet. Then the pastor's wife began to say softly, 'Praise the Lord, praise the Lord,' and praises began rolling from her lips. She continued in this spirit of praise for about ten minutes. Finally, one by one all of us picked it up until we were all praising God. In the midst of that atmosphere the child's convulsions ceased and he fell asleep.

"We stood around for awhile rejoicing

in the Lord. Then while we were talking the child awakened and went back into convulsions. We became alarmed and started to pray and rebuke the devil. We anointed the child with oil and laid hands on him. We went through all the usual maneuvers again, but nothing seemed to help.

"Then when we settled down again, the pastor's wife began to praise the Lord, ministering to the Lord and telling Him how much she loved Him. We all joined in and shortly the child's convulsions stopped and he went to sleep, permanently healed. That night I witnessed the power of praise."

This is an instance in which the prayer of worship worked when nothing else did. As these Christians, like those in the Early Church, "ministered to the Lord," the Holy Ghost moved and made manifest the mighty power of God. ⚔

MEMORY TEXT:

"And they worshipped him, and returned to Jerusalem with great joy: And were continually in the temple, praising and blessing God."
(Luke 24:52-53)

THE LESSON IN ACTION: *"But be ye doers of the word, and not hearers only..."* James 1:22

This week I will put the lesson into practice by doing the following:

Lesson 13

The Prayer of Worship
(Part II)

Acts 16:22-25
II Chronicles 20:15, 17-19, 21-22
Luke 24:50-53

In the sixteenth chapter of Acts we have the story of Paul and Silas in Philippi. We read of their arrest, how they were beaten with many stripes and cast into prison.

ACTS 16:22-25

22 And the multitude rose up together against them: and the magistrates rent off their clothes, and commanded to beat them.

23 And when they had laid many stripes upon them, they cast them into prison, charging the jailer to keep them safely.

24 Who, having received such a charge, thrust them into the inner prison, and made their feet fast in the stocks.

25 And at midnight, Paul and Silas prayed, and sang praises unto God: and the prisoners heard them.

A Song at Midnight

I want to call special attention to verse 25, ". . . Paul and Silas prayed, and sang praises unto God . . ." What did they have to be so happy about that they felt like singing? Surely nothing was going right for them. They had been out preaching the good news of the gospel and what did they get for it? They were brought before the rulers, were charged and beaten, and then were cast into prison with their feet placed in stocks.

Their backs were sore and bleeding. Every part of their bodies ached. But did they sit there moaning and complaining, crying, "Why did this have to happen to me?" No. The Bible says they "sang praises unto God."

If they had been like some of us today the scripture might have read, "And at midnight Paul and Silas griped and complained, whined and whimpered, wondering why God has allowed this to come upon them." Their conversation might have followed this line:

"Paul, you still there?"

"Sure, I'm still here. Where else could I be?"

"I tell you, my poor back is really hurting me. I just don't understand why God ever sent this on us. He knows that I've tried to serve Him and have done my best."

That kind of attitude would have just gotten them further into trouble instead of out of it.

We can learn something here from Paul and Silas. After all, they were in trouble. They were in pain. They were in jail. All in all, it was a pretty dark picture. One could hardly blame them for being discouraged. However, as someone has said, Paul and Silas got in jail but they didn't let the jail get in them.

This is the reason many people are defeated. Trouble comes to everyone, but our attitude toward it is what makes the difference between victory and defeat. How we look at the situation makes the difference in how we come out or whether we get out at all. In the example of Paul and Silas we can find help for our midnight hour, for our time of testing, in an hour when the storms of life threaten to sweep us overboard.

Paul and Silas weren't in Philippi on a vacation. They were there to do the Lord's work. They weren't out of the will of God. The first thing that some people think when adversity strikes is that they must surely be out of the Lord's will or such a thing wouldn't have happened. But Paul and Silas were right in the middle of God's will. If we were to measure whether we are in God's will by whether everything runs smoothly with no hard places and no sacrifices, then Paul never did get in the will of God in his entire ministry. He missed it from beginning to end.

Let us notice something else in verse 25. "And at midnight Paul and Silas prayed, and sang praises unto God: *and the prisoners heard them."* They weren't quiet about it. They were praising God out loud right there in jail. Not only did the prisoners hear them, but God heard them! "And suddenly there was a great earthquake, so that the foundations of the prison were shaken: and immediately all the doors were opened and every one's bands were loosed" (Verse 26).

Deliverance came while they were praising God.

A Song in Battle

Let us look at the Old Testament counterpart to this story. During the reign of King Jehoshaphat, the Ammonites and Moabites came against the Israelites. Jehoshaphat cried out to the Lord in prayer and He answered him.

II CHRONICLES 20:15, 17–19, 21–22

15 And he said, Hearken ye, all Judah, and ye inhabitants of Jerusalem, and thou king Jehoshaphat, Thus saith the Lord unto you, Be not afraid nor dismayed by reason of this great multitude; for the battle is not yours, but God's.

17 Ye shall not need to fight in this battle; set yourselves, stand ye still, and see the salvation of the Lord with you, O Judah and Jerusalem: fear not, nor be dismayed; to morrow go out against them: for the Lord will be with you.

18 And Jehoshaphat bowed his head with his face to the ground: and all Judah and the inhabitants of Jerusalem fell before the Lord, worshipping the Lord.

19 And the Levites, of the children of the Kohathites, and of the children of the Korhites, stood up to praise the Lord God of Israel with a loud voice on high.

21 And when he had consulted with the people, he appointed singers unto the Lord, and that should praise the beauty of holiness, as they went out before the army, and to say, Praise the Lord; for his mercy endureth for ever.

22 And when they began to sing and to praise, the Lord set ambushments against the children of Ammon, Moab, and mount Seir, which were come against Judah; and they were smitten.

Jehoshaphat knew that his army was no match for those of the countries banded against him. But he knew his God was more than a match for them. He called a prayer meeting and they fasted and prayed. The Spirit of God moved upon a young man in the congregation and he stood and prophesied. The Lord told them not to fear, for the battle was the Lord's.

The next morning when they went out against the enemy's powerful armies, they did not go against them with swords and spears but with songs of praise (Verse 21). They marched along and chanted, "Praise the Lord; for his mercy endureth for ever." They sang and praised the Lord just as Paul and Silas did in jail. In their hour of trial, instead of cowering in fear the children of Israel sang praises to God just as Paul and Silas did.

And what was the outcome of this battle? Look at verse 22. "And when they began to sing and to praise, the Lord sent ambushments against the children of Ammon, Moab, and mount Seir, which were come against Judah; and they were smitten." When they began to sing praises unto God, He did something. They witnessed a manifestation of God's power.

Praise, a Characteristic of the Early Church

A spirit of praise and rejoicing was a characteristic of the early church.

LUKE 24:50–53

50 And he led them out as far as to Bethany, and he lifted up his hands, and blessed them.

51 And it came to pass, while he blessed them, he was parted from them, and carried up into heaven.

52 And they worshipped him, and returned to Jerusalem with great joy:

53 And were continually in the temple, praising and blessing God.

After the disciples watched Jesus return to heaven, they went back to Jerusalem with hearts filled with praise and thanksgiving to God.

Then we read about them in Acts 2:46–47, "And they, continuing daily with one accord in the temple, and breaking bread from house to house, did eat their meat with gladness and singleness of heart, Praising God, and having favour with all the people. And the Lord added to the church daily such as should be saved." Notice the expression, "They, continuing daily with one accord . . . eat their meat with gladness . . . praising God . . ." With these early Christians this wasn't only a spasmodic occurrence. It wasn't just something that happened once in a great while. The Bible uses the words "continually" and "daily."

Too many times some Christians today will get prayed through about once every six months and will have a time of praising and blessing God. If we were writing about them we would have to use the words "occasionally" or perhaps even "semi-annually." But of the early Christians the Bible records that they "were continually in the temple, praising and blessing God."

If we want to see the same manifestations of *power* that the early church had, we are going to have to see the same manifestations of *praise* that they had.

THE LESSON IN ACTION: *"But be ye doers of the word, and not hearers only . . ."* James 1:22

This week I will put the lesson into practice by doing the following:

Lesson 14

United Prayer

Acts 4:23-31

In the third chapter of Acts we read that as Peter and John entered the temple through the gate called Beautiful, they saw a man begging alms. Peter told the man to look on them. Expecting to receive a coin, he looked at them. Peter said to him, "Silver and gold have I none; but such as I have give I thee: In the name of Jesus Christ of Nazareth rise up and walk" (Acts 3:6). Peter took the man by the hand, lifted him up and the man started walking. He went into the temple praising God.

This raised a stir among the people, and Peter and John were brought before the priests and elders. They were cast into prison and the next day were brought before the rulers. Unable to deny that a true miracle had taken place, the priests were forced to let them go. However, they commanded them not to preach or teach in the name of Jesus anymore. Then we read:

ACTS 4:23–30

23 And being let go, they went to their own company, and reported all that the chief priests and elders had said unto them.

24 And when they heard that, they lifted up their voice to God with one accord, and said, Lord, thou art God, which hast made heaven, and earth, and the sea, and all that in them is:

25 Who by the mouth of thy servant David hast said, Why did the heathen rage, and the people imagine vain things?

26 The kings of the earth stood up, and the rulers were gathered together against the Lord, and against his Christ.

27 For of a truth against thy holy child Jesus, whom thou hast anointed, both Herod, and Pontius Pilate, with the Gentiles, and the people of Israel, were gathered together,

28 For to do whatsoever thy hand and thy counsel determined before to be done.

29 And now, Lord, behold their threatenings: and grant unto thy servants, that with all boldness they may speak thy word.

30 By stretching forth thine hand to heal; and that signs and wonders may be done by the name of thy holy child Jesus.

From Prison to Prayer Group

Notice the first thing Peter and John did when they were released from the prison. "And being let go, they went to their own company . . . ." A good place to be when in trouble is with your "own company," people of like faith. It is good to be around people who know how to pray.

I have often thought that if this group had been like some Christians today, the first thing they would have done would have been to organize a committee to go talk to these leaders and make some kind of a deal whereby everyone could get along together. After all, these leaders were religious men, too. They believed in God and prayer. They believed in going to church. The only difference was just that they didn't accept Jesus as being the Messiah, the Son of God.

However, the Bible does not say that they appointed a committee for compro-

55

mise. It says, "they lifted up their voice to God with one accord . . . ." They knew the value of united prayer.

I was raised in a Southern Baptist church and in my youth I never heard people praying aloud in united prayer. In our church someone usually led in prayer. We never lifted our voices as a group in prayer.

Later when I started attending some Full Gospel services, their praying all at once disturbed me. I would go down to the altar to pray with them, but I prayed quietly. It bothered me because they prayed aloud. Their services stimulated my faith, but when I prayed at the altar I would get at the far end, away from them, so I wouldn't be close to their noise.

One time I ventured to say something about it. I told them that God wasn't hard of hearing. They responded, "He isn't nervous, either."

I decided to search my Bible for the scriptural answer to this question. I wanted to see how the early church prayed. We claim to be preaching the same new birth they preached, so we might as well be following them in prayer also. As I read through the book of Acts, I underlined in red pencil every verse where it said that the people prayed in a group with two or more praying. I couldn't find one place where they would call on one person to lead in prayer. Nor did they have any kind of sentence prayers or anything like that. I found that the Bible said they lifted their voices. They all prayed at once, and they all prayed out loud.

After reading this, the next time I went to a Full Gospel service I got right in the middle of where they were praying. After my mind had been renewed with the Word, I got blessed with a blessing such as I had never had before when I had prayed alone quietly. I saw for the first time the blessing of united prayer.

Results of United Prayer

What was the result of the united prayer of the believers in this fourth chapter of Acts? Let's look at verse 31:

Acts 4:31

31 And when they had prayed, the place was shaken where they were assembled together; and they were all filled with the Holy Ghost, and they spake the word of God with boldness.

Had their united prayer been answered? In verse 29 we read that they had prayed, "And now, Lord, behold their threatenings: and grant unto thy servants, that with all boldness they may speak thy word." They had not asked the Lord to remove the persecution or to strike down their enemies. They had not asked the Lord to make their way easy. Instead they prayed that in the midst of persecution they might preach the word with boldness. And the Lord answered their prayer.

Verse 31 says that ". . . the place was shaken where they were assembled together . . . ." Do you know of any group of people who are praying and shaking anything nowadays? If Christians today could get together and pray "with one accord" they could shake the world for Jesus. There is power in united prayer.

Notice too that their prayer was for something specific. They were definite in their praying. They were not just praying some generalized prayer, but were praying about the need that faced them right then. And they all prayed at once. As they lifted their voices to God in fervent prayer, "the place was shaken."

In our last lesson we studied about a very similar incident. Paul and Silas had been thrown in jail in Philippi for preaching the gospel. Instead of complaining to the Lord for what had happened to them, they lifted their voices to the Lord in songs of praise. "And at midnight Paul and Silas prayed, and sang praises unto

God: and the prisoners heard them" (Acts 16:25). They too were praying aloud, for *"the prisoners heard them."* They weren't off in some corner mumbling quietly forlorn pleas to God. ". . . The prisoners heard them" as they "sang praises unto God."

Some people say that they want to pray quietly because the Lord knows they have a song in their heart. But if it is there, it is going to come out, ". . . For out of the abundance of the heart the mouth speaketh" (Matt. 12:34).

Did God answer the united prayer of Paul and Silas? Acts 16:26 says, "And suddenly there was a great earthquake, so that the foundations of the prison were shaken: and immediately all the doors were opened and every one's bands were loosed." Again the place was shaken as a result of united prayer!

When Paul and Silas joined forces in prayer and praise to God, the very foundations of the prison were shaken. The stocks came off their feet and they were free. The jailer, awakened by the earthquake, saw the prison doors standing open and assumed the prisoners had fled.

He knew he would be held responsible for their escape, and he became so frightened that he was going to kill himself. Just then Paul cried out, ". . . Do thyself no harm: for we are all here" (Verse 28).

The jailer knew he had witnessed the supernatural that night. He knew Paul and Silas were no ordinary men, and he ". . . came trembling, and fell down before Paul and Silas, And brought them out, and said, Sirs, what must I do to be saved? And they said, Believe on the Lord Jesus Christ, and thou shalt be saved, and thy house" (Verses 29-31). As a result of Paul's and Silas' united prayer that night, the jailer, together with his entire family, accepted Christ as Saviour and were all baptized.

There is supernatural power in united prayer. ⚔

MEMORY TEXT:

"These all continued with one accord in prayer and supplication..:."
(Acts 1:14)

THE LESSON IN ACTION: *"But be ye doers of the word, and not hearers only..."* James 1:22

This week I will put the lesson into practice by doing the following:

When the winds of adversity blow, we can do exactly as the Word of God says. We do not have to fret or worry, we can cast our burdens on the Lord.

The Prayer of Commitment

Matthew 6:25-27
Philippians 4:6

Do you sometimes pray about a problem with seemingly no results? Unanswered prayers are usually due to our not praying in line with the Word of God.

There are often times when we need to pray the prayer of commitment. Peter talked about this kind of prayer when he said, "Casting all your care upon him: for he careth for you" (I Peter 5:7). I believe the Amplified translation is most illuminating and enlightening on this particular verse. It says, "Casting the whole of your care—all your anxieties, all your worries, all your concerns, once and for all—on Him; for He cares for you affectionately, and cares about you watchfully."

How wonderful it is that we can cast our cares upon the Lord in prayer.

Pray According to Laws Governing Prayer

If people would just pray this prayer of commitment, it would eliminate some of the things they are praying about. Some people's prayers are not answered because they are not doing what God said to do about cares, anxieties, worries and concerns. It is not going to do any good to pray about your cares unless you do what God tells you to do about them.

Some Christians seem satisfied just to think that God knows and understands all about their problems—but they still cling to their cares. Therefore, they don't get deliverance. It is not enough to know that He understands and is concerned. We must go on and do what He said to do if we want deliverance from our problems. Cast all of your cares, all of your anxieties, all of your worries upon Him for He cares for you.

This is the prayer of commitment, the prayer of casting or rolling our cares and burdens upon Him. A scripture in the Psalms may help us to see a little more clearly what Peter is talking about here. "Commit thy way unto the Lord; trust also in him; and he shall bring it to pass" (Psalm 37:5). The reference in the King James version says, "Roll thy way upon the Lord." Commit, cast, roll your burden on the Lord. He is not going to take it away from you. Some request, "Pray that the Lord will lighten this load." He's not going to do that. He doesn't want to just lighten your load. He wants to *carry* it all. But there is a vital part that we must play in this. It is the prayer of *commitment*.

God does not want His children to worry, to be full of anxiety or burdened down with the cares of life. But there is something which you must do. In an imperative sentence, such as those in I Peter 5:7 and Psalm 37:5, the subject of the sentence is understood to be "you." The Lord said, *"(You)* cast all your care upon him . . ." *"(You)* commit thy way unto the Lord . . ." We must do our part, we must obey the Lord, before He can come to our aid. We must turn loose of our problem before He can take over.

This is a once-and-for-all proposition—it isn't something that you do every day. When we really *cast* our cares upon Him, when we really commit our way unto the Lord, we don't have them anymore. We are rid of them. They are no longer in our hands, but in His. There is so much that the Lord would have done for us, but we wouldn't let Him. We may have been honest and sincere in our praying about some matters, but we saw no answers to our prayers because we did not come according to His rules, according to His laws that govern the operation of prayer. We did not do what He told us to do, yet we wondered why He didn't work certain things out for us.

Sometimes we have brought our burden to the altar of prayer. We have prayed and prayed and prayed about it. Then when we got up to leave, we picked up our burden off the altar and took it home with us.

Too, there are those who do not really want to get rid of their problems. Oh, they claim, sometimes rather loudly, that they do. But they don't, not really; for if they did, they wouldn't have anything to get people's sympathy. They wouldn't have anything to complain about. They would almost have to close down conversation.

The Futility of Worry

MATTHEW 6:25-27

25 Therefore I say unto you, Take no thought for your life, what ye shall eat, or what ye shall drink; nor yet for your body, what ye shall put on. Is not the life more than meat, and the body than raiment?

26 Behold the fowls of the air: for they sow not, neither do they reap, nor gather into barns; yet your heavenly Father feedeth them. Are ye not much better than they?

27 Which of you by taking thought can add one cubit unto his stature?

Jesus was simply saying in this passage of scripture, "Which of you by worrying and being over-anxious is going to change anything?" We all know that worry is like a rocking chair—it keeps you busy, but doesn't get you anywhere.

Luke's gospel records the same portion

above and says, "And he said unto his disciples, Therefore, I say unto you, Take no thought for your life . . ." (Luke 12: 22). Another translation of this verse reads, "Be not anxious about tomorrow."

Of course, we have to plan and prepare for tomorrow. We have to make certain provisions for the future. But what the Lord was teaching us here is that He doesn't want us to be filled with anxiety and worry about tomorrow. We can say with the gospel songwriter, "I don't know about tomorrow, but I know who holds my hand." That's all that is important.

Worry Nullifies Prayer

PHILIPPIANS 4:6

6 Be careful for nothing; but in every thing by prayer and supplication with thanksgiving let your requests be made known unto God.

The Amplified translation of this verse will help us. It says, "Do not fret or have any anxiety about anything." Again, "you" is the understood subject of the sentence. When the Lord said, "Be careful (anxious) for nothing," He was saying, "(You) be careful for nothing . . ." In other words, "Don't *you* fret or have any anxiety about anything."

As long as you are going to fret and have anxiety concerning the thing you are praying about, you are nullifying the effects of your praying. You haven't cast it on the Lord, you still have it. If you have it, He doesn't have it. If He has it, you don't have it.

As long as you are still worrying about your problem, lying awake at night, tossing from one side of the bed to the other trying to figure it out, He doesn't have it. As long as your stomach churns every time you think about it, as long as you can't eat for worrying about it, He doesn't have it. You do. And really all of your praying about it will not work because you have not done as He has commanded. He has promised to "bring it to pass," but only after you have committed your "way unto the Lord."

When we cast our cares on the Lord, we no longer have them. To illustrate, if I took the last five dollars out of my billfold and gave it to you, I wouldn't have it anymore, you would. Then if someone came along and asked to borrow a dollar, promising to pay it back the next day, I would have to say, "I don't have a dollar." I had just given my money to you I wouldn't have it, you would.

I pastored for about twelve years, and occasionally during that time problems arose and I would be tempted to worry about them. When I would find myself becoming anxious about something I would start talking to myself. "Now Kenneth," I would say, "you know better than this. You are beginning to fret. Don't do it. It's not right."

Many times during the night I would awaken and the devil would bring to my mind a picture of certain conditions which existed in the church. I would be tempted to worry, but instead of worrying, I'd start laughing right out loud and say, "I don't have that problem. Praise the Lord, I'm carefree. I don't have it, devil. You can show me a picture of it if you want, but I don't have it. The Lord has it."

It is amazing what God can do with your problems when He has them. But as long as you hold onto them, as long as you try to figure it out for Him and try to help Him work it out, then He

doesn't have any of it. You have it all.

When the winds of adversity blow, we can do exactly as the Word of God says. We do not have to fret or worry, we can cast our burdens on the Lord. If you haven't done it yet, there is no better time than now to turn loose of your problem and sleep peacefully tonight. If the devil tries to bring a picture of it before you, put it out of your mind immediately and say, "No, I don't have that, devil. I don't have a care, I have turned it over to the Lord and He has it."

He'll work on it while you are sleeping. He never slumbers or sleeps (Psalm 121:4). You need sleep, but He doesn't. ". . . He giveth his beloved sleep (Psalm 127:2). You are His beloved because you are accepted in the Beloved, the Lord Jesus Christ (Ephesians 1:6). Therefore, you can sleep peacefully.

If we really believe the Bible and practice God's Word, then we should never worry. If we really believe what Jesus said, "If ye shall ask any thing in my name, I will do it" (John 14:14), then we wouldn't worry even if when we went home we found our house had burned down while we were gone. We wouldn't worry or fret about it, we would say, "Praise God, we'll get a better one." This is the place God wants us to be. Purpose in your heart today to practice God's Word, to practice faith. ⚔

MEMORY TEXT:

"Casting all your care upon him; for he careth for you." (I Peter 5:7)

THE LESSON IN ACTION: *"But be ye doers of the word, and not hearers only . . ."* James 1:22

This week I will put the lesson into practice by doing the following:

Lesson 16

What Jesus Said About Prayer

(Part I)

Matthew 6:5-13

While Jesus was here on earth He taught much about prayer. Perhaps the best known of His teachings on prayer is the oft repeated "Lord's Prayer." In this brief prayer we find a pattern for prayer which Jesus gave to His disciples. Just preceding this prayer, as recorded in Matthew's gospel, are a few verses which are also very enlightening on this subject, and are really a prelude to the prayer.

MATTHEW 6:5-13

5 And when thou prayest, thou shalt not be as the hypocrites are: for they love to pray standing in the synagogues and in the corners of the streets, that they may be seen of men. Verily I say unto you, They have their reward.

6 But thou, when thou prayest, enter into thy closet, and when thou hast shut thy door, pray to thy Father which is in secret; and thy Father which seeth in secret shall reward thee openly.

7 But when ye pray, use not vain repetitions, as the heathen do: for they think that they shall be heard for their much speaking.

8 Be not ye therefore like unto them: for your Father knoweth what things ye have need of, before ye ask him.

9 After this manner therefore pray ye: Our Father which art in heaven, Hallowed be thy name.

10 Thy kingdom come. Thy will be done in earth, as it is in heaven.

11 Give us this day our daily bread.

12 And forgive us our debts, as we forgive our debtors.

13 And lead us not into temptation, but deliver us from evil: For thine is the kingdom, and the power, and the glory, for ever. Amen.

Private Prayer

One of the first things Jesus said here was, "And when thou prayest, thou shalt not be as the hypocrites are . . . ." Surely none of us wants to be hypocritical, especially in our praying. Then He described the hypocrite—". . . They love to pray standing in the synagogues and in the corners of the streets, that they may be seen of men."

This does not mean that all of our praying should be private. As we looked at the early church in prayer in Lesson 14, we saw them praying together as a group throughout the book of Acts. What Jesus was referring to here was the danger of praying only to be seen of men. There are those who just pray in public to appear really spiritual, to make people think they are real prayer warriors. Those who pray only for the applause of men have their reward, and that is all it is— the fleeting applause of men.

Jesus told His disciples to "enter into thy closet, and when thou hast shut thy door, pray to thy Father which is in secret." He was stressing the importance of a private prayer life. Public prayer is necessary and vital in the life of the church. Praying together as a family is vital and necessary to the spiritual strength of the home. But private prayer is essential to the spiritual life of the individual. This is when we grow in spiritual stature. This should not be just those crisis times when we are driven to our knees. We should be spiritually prepared for such times through a daily prayer time which we set aside for fellowship with God.

Repetitious Prayer

Jesus went on to say, "But when ye pray, use not vain repetitions, as the heathen do: for they think that they shall be heard for their much speaking" (Verse 7). We have two admonitions from the Lord: (1) Don't be like the hypocrites in our praying, and (2) Don't be like the heathen in our praying. Jesus said that the heathen think they will be heard by their gods because of their repetitious praying, because of their much speaking.

Sad to say, some of this heathen thinking has sifted down into Christian thinking. Many have the idea that God will hear them because of their much speaking, their lengthy and repeated calling on God. They repeat the same prayer, they say the same phrases and words over and over again, thinking they will be heard because of that. But this is exactly what Jesus condemned when He said, ". . . Use not vain repetitions, as the heathen do . . . ."

Then He said, "Be not ye therefore like unto them: for your Father knoweth what things ye have need of, before ye ask him." He knows before you ask, but yet He wants you to ask, as we shall see in the next chapter of Matthew, because He said, "Ask, and it shall be given you . . . ." (Matt. 7:7).

God does not hear you simply because you repeat the same prayer over and over. Some seem to have the idea that if they could just pray long enough and loudly enough, eventually they could talk God into hearing them. God is not going to hear you because you prayed loudly or because you prayed quietly. As we have seen in previous lessons, it is the prayer of faith that God hears. He hears you because you believe Him when you pray, and come according to His Word

Basic Principles of Prayer

In the next few verses in Matthew, Jesus taught His disciples some basic elements of prayer. Commonly referred to as the Lord's Prayer, it is more accurately the Disciples' Prayer or the model for prayer that He gave to them while He walked with them on the earth. Certainly, dispensationally speaking, this is not the Church praying, for they did not ask anything in the name of Jesus. When the Church prays, they pray in the name of Jesus. However, we can learn many truths concerning prayer here.

Jesus was not telling the disciples to pray this prayer word for word. He was giving them some principles in connection with prayer that will work for the Church today.

The Principle of Praise

The prayer began with the words, "Our Father which art in heaven . . ." The unsaved can pray this prayer with their lips just as anyone can recite a poem, a prayer, or sing a song. But to really pray this prayer from the heart, to really have fellowship with God, one must actually be a child of God. Otherwise, he cannot truly say, "Our Father . . ."

We hear much teaching these days about the "fatherhood of God and the brotherhood of man." Some would try to make us believe that we are all children of God, that He is the Father of all of us. It is true that He is the Creator of all and we are all fellow creatures, but God isn't the Father of all of us. He is only the Father of those who have been born again, those who are in His family.

During Jesus' earthly ministry He once said to a group of Pharisees, who were very religious people, "Ye are of your father the devil" (John 8:44). The Pharisees were good people as far as works were concerned. Yet Jesus said to them, "Ye are of your father the devil." In order to be able to address God as Father, we must be born again. He is more than our God; He is our Father.

Jesus is saying here that the right approach to God is to come to Him because He is our Father, and to come in praise and in worship. "Our Father which art in heaven, Hallowed be thy name" (Verse 9). Come first with praise. Come first with worship into His presence, because He is our Father.

The Principle of Putting God First

The next verse in this pattern prayer says, "Thy kingdom come, Thy will be done in earth, as it in heaven" (Verse 10). The principle involved here is that of putting the kingdom of God first. Later on in this same chapter Jesus repeated this principle. "But seek ye first the kingdom of God, and his righteousness; and all these things shall be added unto you" (Verse 33). If we put God first, we need have no worry about material needs, for "all these things shall be added unto you." We do not have to go through life with the soles of our shoes worn thin, with unpaid bills past due, and driving an old Model T Ford. If God is first in our lives, "all these things shall be added."

Have you ever thought how all-inclusive this prayer is? He prayed, "Thy kingdom come, *Thy will be done in earth, as it is in heaven.*" Do you suppose there are any sick folks in heaven? No. Nor is it

God's will that there should be any sick folk on earth. God wants to shower our lives with blessings. He wants our lives here on earth to be lived in the center of His will, as it is in heaven. He wants us to enjoy abundant living. ". . . I am come that they might have life, and that they might have it more abundantly" (John 10:10).

The Principle of Daily Prayer

In the next verse of this prayer Jesus taught us the importance of daily prayer, of asking Him for our every need. "Give us this day our *daily* bread" (Verse 11). Even though He knows our every need, He still wants us to ask Him.

The Principle of Forgiveness

Jesus taught much about forgiveness during His stay here on earth, and He included it here as one of the essential elements of prayer. "And forgive us our debts, as we forgive our debtors" (Verse 12). In verses 14–15 He also said, "For if ye forgive men their trespasses, your heavenly Father will also forgive you: But if ye forgive not men their trespasses, neither will your Father forgive your trespasses." Prayer will not work in an unforgiving heart. We simply cannot hold a grudge against anyone and maintain a real prayer life that gets results.

There are many instances where mental confusion and emotional frustration can be attributed to harboring bitterness against others. Doctors have learned that people who hold resentment in their hearts are more susceptible to certain types of diseases. When they could get such patients to rid themselves of their resentment, although they had not responded at all to medical treatment, in most cases their trouble cleared up. More and more, medical science is discovering how closely related our inner feelings are to our physical health.

According to Romans 5:17 God's plan is for us to reign in life by Christ Jesus—to reign over circumstances, poverty, disease, everything that would hinder us.

I have sometimes heard Christians (who, mind you, were not walking in the closest fellowship with the Lord) tell me how badly they had been treated by a certain person. They would say, "Oh, yes, I have forgiven him all right. But I never will forget what he did to me." They really hadn't forgiven that person at all. Resentment still lurked in the hidden corners of their heart.

The Principle of Deliverance From Temptation

"And lead us not into temptation, but deliver us from evil . . ."(Verse 13). The word temptation means *test* or *trial*. Many tests and trials could be met in advance by a child of God enjoying the fellowship with the Father that a proper prayer life brings.

Then we come to the conclusion. ". . . For thine is the kingdom, and the power, and the glory, for ever. Amen" (Verse 13). The prayer that began with praise also ends with praise. ⚕

MEMORY TEXT:

"But seek ye first the kingdom of God, and his righteousness; and all these things shall be added unto you." *(Matt. 6:33)*

THE LESSON IN ACTION: *"But be ye doers of the word, and not hearers only . . ."* James 1:22

This week I will put the lesson into practice by doing the following:

God loves us and wants us to have good things just as we love our children and want them to have good things.

Lesson 17

What Jesus Said About Prayer
(Part II)

Matthew 7:7-11; Luke 11:5-13

The model prayer which Jesus gave to His disciples, commonly referred to as the Lord's Prayer (Matt. 6:9–13), begins with the words, "Our Father which art in heaven ...."

In the next chapter of Matthew when Jesus is again teaching on prayer, He uses another illustration of how the earthly relationship between father and son is like the believer's relationship with the heavenly Father.

MATTHEW 7:7–11

7 Ask, and it shall be given you; seek, and ye shall find; knock, and it shall be opened unto you:

8 For every one that asketh receiveth; and he that seeketh findeth; and to him that knocketh it shall be opened.

9 Or what man is there of you, whom if his son ask bread, will he give him a stone?

10 Or if he ask a fish, will he give him a serpent?

11 If ye then, being evil, know how to give good gifts unto your children, how much more shall your Father which is in heaven give good things to them that ask him?

Knowing God as Father

We can see here one reason the Jews could not understand Jesus. If He had come along as did some of the prophets of old, proclaiming judgment against them and presenting to them a distant, unapproachable God, they might have better understood Him. That was the picture of God they were accustomed to. When God came down and talked to Moses on the mountain, there was fire, thunder and lightning; and if anyone touched that mountain he died instantly. When the presence of God moved into the Holy of Holies, no one dared intrude there for fear of instant death. The Jews knew about a God who was high and holy, who dealt an awful judgment; and they feared Him.

Jesus, however, came with a message of love. He introduced God as a Father and suggested that they could approach God as a Father. But the Jews just couldn't comprehend that kind of a God.

We see the same thing today. To many, Christianity is just a religion about a far away God. They don't really know Him. They have never come to Him through Jesus Christ in order to know Him personally as their Father, and so they try to approach Him in the wrong manner.

But thank God, He is our Father and we can come to Him because we are His children.

Ask, Seek, Knock . . . Believe

Most Christians are aware that this verse is in the Bible, whether or not they use it. "Ask, and it shall be given you; seek, and ye shall find; knock, and it shall be opened unto you" (Verse 7). Too often, though, we fail to receive what we are asking for, we fail to find what we are seeking; and the door on which we are knocking is not opened. Why? We must be doing something wrong when we don't receive, for the next verse promises, "For every one that asketh receiveth; and he that seeketh findeth; and to him that knocketh it shall be opened" (Verse 8). What is the reason for our failure?

65

I once read a book by a missionary who spent 32 years in the Holy Land. This was around the turn of the century when customs there were very much like they had been for centuries before. In his book the missionary commented on this passage of scripture in Matthew 7:7-8. He said, "I thought, as most Christians do, that when Jesus said, 'Ask, and it shall be given you; seek, and ye shall find; knock, and it shall be opened unto you,' that He meant if you asked and didn't receive an immediate answer to keep on asking. However, after living in the Holy Land for so many years and becoming familiar with the thinking of the Eastern mind, I learned that this was not what Jesus meant at all.

"In those days if someone came to the outer gate and knocked, seeking entrance, the more wealthy would send their servant to call out and ask the name of the visitor. If it was someone who was known, they could enter immediately. If it was someone unknown the servant would go to the master of the house and ask if he should let the visitor in. The thought here is that when you knock, if you are known, you gain immediate entrance. 'To him that knocketh it shall be opened.' "

If when we ask we do not receive, if when we seek we do not find, if when we knock it is not opened to us, we should first ask ourselves if we are known by the Master of the house. If not, we should become acquainted, personally and intimately, with our Lord and Saviour Jesus Christ. We should make Him Lord of our life.

Having done this, the next step is faith, to "believe that he is, and that he is a rewarder of them that diligently seek him" (Heb. 11:6). For, as Jesus explained in Matthew 7:11, our heavenly Father is eager to give good gifts unto His children. "If ye then, being evil, know how to give good gifts unto your children,

how much more shall your Father which is in heaven give good things to them that ask him?" (Verse 11).

What earthly father wants his children to go through life poor and downtrodden, sick and suffering? On the contrary, most of us labor and sacrifice so that our children can have advantages that we ourselves never had. So if you, being carnal, being human, want good things for your children, *"how much more* shall your Father which is in heaven give good things to them that ask him? Those three words, "how much more," send a thrill through my spirit. If we want happiness for our children, *how much more* does God want the same for us. If we want good health for our children, *how much more* does God want good health for us. If we want material blessings for our children, *how much more* does God want the same for us.

Luke's account of this story gives us a few more details.

LUKE 11:5-13

5 And he said unto them, Which of you shall have a friend, and shall go unto him at midnight, and say unto him, Friend, lend me three loaves:

6 For a friend of mine in his journey is come to me, and I have nothing to set before him?

7 And he from within shall answer and say, Trouble me not: the door is now shut, and my children are with me in bed; I cannot rise and give thee.

8 I say unto you, Though he will not rise and give him, because he is his friend, yet because of his importunity he will rise and give him as many as he needeth.

9 And I say unto you, Ask, and it shall be given you; seek, and ye shall find; knock, and it shall be opened unto you.

10 For every one that asketh receiveth; and he that seeketh findeth; and to him that knocketh it shall be opened.

11 If a son shall ask bread of any of you that is a father, will he give him a stone? or if he ask a fish, will he for a fish give him a serpent?

12 Or if he shall ask an egg, will he offer him a scorpion?

13 If ye then, being evil, know how to give good gifts unto your children: how much more shall your heavenly Father give the Holy Spirit to them that ask him?

The Prayer of Importunity

In this account which deals with the prayer of importunity, many people have had the mistaken idea that Jesus was teaching us to keep on asking in order to get results. In this parable we see a man who had a guest arrive during the night. As he didn't have any bread to set before him, he went to his neighbor's house and asked for a loaf of bread. The neighbor responded, "I'm already in bed, don't bother me." But when the man kept pleading with him he finally granted his request.

Jesus was illustrating here that although the neighbor would not get out of bed to give the man bread just because he was a friend, yet because of his importunity he gave it to him. Jesus was saying yet *how much more* our heavenly Father will hear us and grant our requests.

It is the importunity of faith, not the importunity of unbelief that gets results. We can keep on begging God, importuning all we want, and we will never get an answer if our importuning prayer is in unbelief. It is the importunity of faith that works. "Ask, and it shall be given you; seek, and ye shall find; knock, and it shall be opened unto you."

Andrew Murray had real insight into this subject of importunity in prayer. He said that it is not good taste to ask the Lord for the same thing over and over again. He said that if the thing which you have prayed about hasn't materialized, don't ask again the same way you

did in the beginning. That would be a confession that you didn't believe God the first time. Just remind Him of your request. Remind Him of what He promised. Remind Him that you are expecting the answer, and let this importunity be an importunity of faith. That will bring results.

Luke's account of this story is more detailed than Matthew's, and in verse 13 Luke added something. Matthew recorded, "If ye then, being evil, know how to give good gifts unto your children, how much more shall your Father which is in heaven give *good things* to them that ask him?" Luke enlarges on this by saying, "If ye then, being evil, know how to give good gifts unto your children: how much more shall your heavenly Father give the *Holy Spirit* to them that ask him?" Although Matthew didn't specifically name the Holy Spirit in this verse, we know that the Holy Spirit is a "good thing."

I am sure that the Holy Spirit had a purpose for inspiring Luke and Matthew to record this as they did. The Holy Spirit, as He inspired Matthew, wanted to stress the good things of life. He wanted us to know that God loves us just as we love our children and want our children to have good things. The Holy Spirit inspired Luke to emphasize the spiritual things that God has for us.

By asking, seeking, and knocking in faith, we can enjoy all the abundant blessings that God has for His children.

MEMORY TEXT:

"Ask, and it shall be given you; seek, and ye shall find; knock, and it shall be opened unto you." *(Matt 7:7)*

THE LESSON IN ACTION: *"But be ye doers of the word, and not hearers only..."* James 1:22

This week I will put the lesson into practice by doing the following:

Lesson 18

What Jesus Said About Prayer

(Part III)

Matthew 21:18-22
Mark 11:12-14, 20-24
John 15:7-8

In Matthew 21 we come to another passage where Jesus taught on prayer. He was talking about faith and prayer. You can't very well talk about faith without talking about prayer, nor can you talk about prayer without talking about faith. They go hand in hand.

Pray, Believe, Receive

MATTHEW 21:18-22

18 Now in the morning as he returned into the city, he hungered.

19 And when he saw a fig tree in the way, he came to it, and found nothing thereon, but leaves only, and said unto it, Let no fruit grow on thee henceforward for ever. And presently the fig tree withered away.

20 And when the disciples saw it, they marvelled, saying, How soon is the fig tree withered away!

21 Jesus answered and said unto them, Verily I say unto you, If ye have faith, and doubt not, ye shall not only do this which is done to the fig tree, but also if ye shall say unto this mountain, Be thou removed, and be thou cast into the sea; it shall be done.

22 And all things, whatsoever ye shall ask in prayer, believing, ye shall receive.

Let's also look at this same account as recorded in Mark's gospel. This is the only reference about prayer in the book of Mark, but he devoted a great deal of attention to this one account. Matthew told the story in five verses whereas Mark gives us nearly twice as many on the same story.

MARK 11:12-14, 20-24

12 And on the morrow, when they were come from Bethany, he was hungry:

13 And seeing a fig tree afar off having leaves, he came, if haply he might find any thing thereon: and when he came to it, he found nothing but leaves; for the time of figs was not yet.

14 And Jesus answered and said unto it, No man eat fruit of thee hereafter for ever. And his disciples heard it.

20 And in the morning, as they passed by, they saw the fig tree dried up from the roots.

21 And Peter calling to remembrance saith unto him, Master, behold, the fig tree which thou cursedst is withered away.

22 And Jesus answering saith unto them, Have faith in God.

23 For verily I say unto you, That whosoever shall say unto this mountain, Be thou removed, and be thou cast into the sea; and shall not doubt in his heart, but shall believe that those things which he saith shall come to pass; he shall have whatsoever he saith.

24 Therefore I say unto you, What things soever ye desire, when ye pray, believe that ye receive them, and ye shall have them.

In studying the Bible it is good to compare the different gospel writers' accounts of the same incidents in the life of Jesus, for in this way we can get different viewpoints. One writer might bring out some details that the others left out.

In Matthew's account of the above story, Jesus said, "And all things whatsoever ye shall ask in prayer, believing, ye shall receive" (Verse 22). Mark put it a little differently. ". . . What things soever ye desire, when ye pray, believe that ye receive them, and ye shall have them" (Verse 24). Both writers gave the basic formula for faith: Pray, believe, receive.

Someone has asked, "But what if you didn't receive?" Then you didn't ask believing, did you? The scripture says that if you pray and believe, you shall receive. "Yes, but maybe it isn't the will of God," they reply. The scripture didn't say anything about that here. We are too quick to use this as an excuse for our unbelief. Jesus said that if you ask in prayer, believing, you shall receive.

"But what if someone asked for ten million oil wells?" you might ask. Well, if you can have faith for ten million oil wells, you will get them. But I doubt very seriously that you could believe that. Don't ask me to agree with you in prayer for them because I don't think I could. However, if you can believe that you will receive ten million oil wells, then you will get them. I have believed sometimes for things that have seemed almost as impossible and have received them. Jesus said it, I believe it. "What things soever ye desire, when ye pray, believe that ye receive them, and ye shall have them."

The Word of Faith

In John's account of what Jesus said about prayer, not one single time does he use the words "faith" or "believe." Let us look at one example:

JOHN 15:7-8

7 If ye abide in me, and my words abide in you, ye shall ask what ye will, and it shall be done unto you.

8 Herein is my Father glorified, that ye bear much fruit; so shall ye be my disciples.

Why was it unnecessary to use the words "faith" or "believe" in this passage of scripture on prayer? This is because there is no problem with faith if His words abide in you. There is only a lack of faith when the Word doesn't abide in you, for if the Word doesn't abide, something else does. If the Word abides in you, then faith abides in you. "So then faith cometh by hearing, and hearing by the word of God" (Rom. 10:17).

A person may be giving mental consent to belief in the Word of God. He could stand up, shake his fist and declare with fervor that he believes in the verbal inspiration of the Bible, that he believes it from cover to cover, from Genesis to Revelation, yet never really have the Word abiding in him at all.

Notice that Jesus didn't just say, "If *ye* abide in me . . ." If He had stopped there, we would automatically have it made as born-again Christians, for with the new birth we do abide in Christ. But the scripture goes on to say, ". . . and my words abide in you . . . ."

The Word is called the "word of faith." "But what saith it? The word is nigh thee, even in thy mouth, and in thy heart: that is, the word of faith, which we preach" (Rom. 10:8). If this Word abides in you, it will cause faith to spring up in your heart.

The Light of the Word

That is the reason the Psalmist of old said, "The entrance of thy words giveth light . . . ." (Psalm 119:130). When we know the Word, we are not praying in the dark. We have light. Again the Psalmist said, "Thy word is a lamp unto my feet, and a light unto my path" (Psalm 119:105). We are not walking in the dark. Our pathway is lighted when we have the Word.

If we have a lighted pathway, we can walk in that light. If there is no action, we are not walking. "But if we walk in the light, as he is in the light, we have fellowship one with another...." (I John 1:7). This doesn't say a thing about *standing* in the light. It says "walk." His Word is a light unto the path that we walk. To walk means action. As we walk in the light that God's Word sheds upon our pathway, we will get results in prayer!

The Psalmist also prayed, "...Quicken thou me according to thy Word" (Psalm 119:25). Jesus said, "If my words abide in you...." He cannot quicken us according to His Word, although He wants to, unless His words abide in us, unless we walk in the light of the Word.

I heard F. F. Bosworth preach when He was seventy-five years old and still active for the Lord. He said, "I always start every morning by saying, "Lord, quicken thou me according to thy Word.' " Then he went on to say what it meant to him to be quickened according to God's Word. He told how he was still in good health at age seventy-five. For all these years he had trusted God and had never had any kind of medication.

Bosworth lived to be eighty-two years old and was busy in the Lord's work up until the end. When the time came for him to die, he knew it was near. He knew in his spirit that the Lord was coming for him. A close friend of his flew to his bedside in Florida. When he arrived Brother Bosworth was sitting up in bed. As he lifted his hand and praised God he said, "Brother, this is the day I have waited for all of my life. I am going home."

He had prayed daily, "Lord, quicken thou me according to thy word," and the Lord quickened him every day until He took him home. Bosworth died without sickness or disease. He just went home to be with the Lord.

God's Word is true whether or not we put it into practice. There are going to be some who will enjoy its fullest benefits. Praise God, I am planning to be one of them! ⚕

MEMORY TEXT:

"If ye abide in me and my words abide in you, ye shall ask what ye will, and it shall be done unto you."
(John 15:7)

THE LESSON IN ACTION: *"But be ye doers of the word, and not hearers only..."* James 1:22

This week I will put the lesson into practice by doing the following:

Whatever our need may be, it is our privilege in Christ to demand that this need be met.

What Jesus Said About Prayer

(Part IV)

John 14:10-14, 16:23-24,.7-11

Let us look into the gospel of John again to see what Jesus had to say about prayer. As strange as it may seem, John does not record anything that the other gospel writers do in regard to prayer. What he does say, the others did not include in their accounts. John said that if everything was written which Jesus said and did, the world itself could not contain the books. But he said he wrote that we might believe that Jesus is the Son of God.

Not all the gospel writers recorded the same thing. Luke recorded part of what Matthew said. Mark recorded only one instance of Jesus' teaching on prayer, as we saw in our last lesson in Mark 11: 12-24 on the cursing of the fig tree. Matthew covered this in Matthew 21. Matthew also talked about the prayer of agreement, which none of the other writers mentioned. ". . . If two of you shall agree on earth as touching any thing that they shall ask, it shall be done for them of my Father which is in heaven" (Matt. 18:19). Actually, we have to put all the accounts together in order to get a clear picture of Jesus' teachings on prayer.

John covers the subject of prayer from an entirely different standpoint. Let us look at two passages of scripture which seem similar but really are quite different.

JOHN 14:10-14

10 Believest thou not that I am in the Father, and the Father in me? the words that I speak unto you I speak not of myself: but the Father that dwelleth in me, he doeth the works.

11 Believe me that I am in the Father, and the Father in me: or else believe me for the very works' sake.

12 Verily, verily, I say unto you, He that believeth on me, the works that I do shall he do also; and greater works than these shall he do; because I go unto my Father.

13 And whatsoever ye shall ask in my name, that will I do, that the Father may be glorified in the Son.

14 If ye shall ask any thing in my name, I will do it.

We have used this scripture in regard to prayer, but Jesus is not talking about prayer here at all, although many people think that He is.

Now let us compare two verses in John 16.

JOHN 16:23-24

23 And in that day ye shall ask me nothing. Verily, verily, I say unto you, Whatsoever ye shall ask the Father in my name, he will give it you.

24 Hitherto have ye asked nothing in my name: ask, and ye shall receive, that your joy may be full.

In this passage of scripture Jesus was talking about something entirely different from what He was talking about in chapter 14. In chapter 16 He said, "Whatsoever ye shall ask the Father in my name, *he* will give it you." But in John 14 He says, "And whatsoever ye shall ask in my name, that will *I* do." He is talking about two different things.

To Demand as Our Right

Let us examine these scriptures in the Greek New Testament. The Greek word here translated "ask" means "demand." Or, "Whatsoever ye shall *demand* in my name, that will I do." We are not demanding it of God. When we pray, we ask of God in Jesus' name. But we are demanding this of the devil. Actually, the Greek is more explicit than the English translation. The Greek reads, "Whatsoever ye shall demand as your right . . ." Not ask as a favor.

Whatever we ask or demand as our right, Jesus said, "I will do it." We have the right to demand Satan to take his hands off our finances if we are having difficulty making ends meet. Whatever our need may be, it is our privilege, our right, in Christ to ask, to demand, that this need be met.

We see an example of this in the book of Acts. Peter and John saw a crippled man begging alms at the gate called Beautiful. Peter stopped and said, "Look on us." The man looked at them, expecting to receive a coin. Peter said, "Silver and gold have I none; but such as I have give I thee: In the name of Jesus Christ of Nazareth rise up and walk" (Acts 3:6).

Peter demanded in Jesus' name that the cripple get up and walk. He didn't pray that God would do it. He knew Jesus had said that whatever we demand, or ask, in His name, He will do it.

Just before Jesus said, "Whatsoever ye shall ask (demand) in my name, that will I do . . . ." He said, ". . . He that believeth on me, the works that I do shall he do also . . . ." Peter was doing the works that Jesus did when he healed the cripple.

Even though we pray for the sick today, and this is certainly scriptural (James 5:14-16), Jesus never prayed for the sick. Jesus said, ". . . the works that I do shall he do also . . . ." If we just prayed for the sick and got results, we wouldn't be doing the works that He did.

He laid hands on the sick, but He never prayed for them. He would command the devil to leave, or He would just say, "Go thy way; and as thou hast believed, so be it done unto thee" (Matt. 8:13).

So when Jesus said in John 14:13, "And whatsoever ye shall ask (demand) in my name, that will I do . . . ." He was not talking about praying to God the Father. He was talking about doing the works that Jesus did.

Greater Works

Not only did Jesus say that we would do the same works that He did, He also said, ". . . And greater works than these shall he do . . . ." Then He went on to tell us why we would do greater works. ". . . Because I go unto my Father." The greater works that the Church can and is doing today are due to the fact that Jesus has gone unto the Father.

JOHN 16:7-11

7 Nevertheless I tell you the truth; It is expedient [profitable, for your best] for you that I go away: for if I go not away, the Comforter will not come unto you; but if I depart, I will send him unto you.

8 And when he is come, he will reprove the world of sin, and of righteousness, and of judgment:

9 Of sin, because they believe not on me;

10 Of righteousness, because I go to my Father, and ye see me no more;

11 Of judgment, because the prince of this world is judged.

What are these greater works? We show men and women how to become born again. "But weren't people saved, or born again, under Jesus' ministry?" someone might ask. They were saved in the same sense that the people in the Old Testament were saved, but they were not born again. The work of the Holy Ghost is necessary in the new birth, and while Jesus was on earth the Holy Ghost had not yet been given. This is why Jesus said, "... It is expedient for you that I go away; for if I go not away, the Comforter will not come unto you; but if I depart, I will send him unto you" (John 16:7).

"But didn't Jesus forgive people's sins while He was here on earth?" someone might say. Yes, but there is a difference between forgiving sins and being born again. After a person is born again, if he sins he can get forgiveness, but he is not born again a second time. If that had been the case we might have been born again thousands of times. The new birth is a greater work than a healing or a miracle.

Secondly, not only were people not born again while Jesus was on earth, we never read in the four gospels, "And the Lord added daily to the church such as should be saved." However, we do see this repeatedly in the book of Acts. This is because there wasn't any church in Jesus' day in the sense that we think of the New Testament Church. The only Body of Christ that was on earth then was His physical body. There were those who believed on Him and who had the promise of that which was to come, but this could only be consummated when the Holy Ghost came to baptize them all into one Body. The Body had to be formed. Today we are the spiritual Body of Christ. The only Body of Christ in the world today is the Church.

Not only was no one born again under the ministry of Jesus, nor were there any added to the Church, but also no one was filled with the Holy Ghost under His ministry. These are the greater works that we do because He went unto the Father.

Praying in Jesus' Name

Comparing now what Jesus said in John 16 regarding prayer, He said, "And in that day ye shall ask me nothing" (Verse 23). When He said "in that day," He was referring to the very day in which we now live, the day of the new covenant, the day of the New Testament.

One translation of this verse reads, "In that day ye shall not pray to me." He told us not to pray to Him, but to pray to the Father in Jesus' name. (See Lesson 3.) "... Whatsoever ye shall ask the Father in my name, he will give it you."

Then He went on to say, "Hitherto have ye asked nothing in my name: ask, and ye shall receive, that your joy may be full" (Verse 24). He was telling them that now, while He was on the earth with them, they do not pray to the Father in His name. But "in that day" when He would no longer be on the earth, they would then ask the Father, in the name of Jesus, "and ye shall receive, that your joy may be full."

Our heavenly Father longs to meet our every need, if only we would ask Him, in order that our "joy may be full." ⚔

MEMORY TEXT:

"If ye shall ask any thing in my name, I will do it." *(John 14:14)*

THE LESSON IN ACTION: *"But be ye doers of the word, and not hearers only..."* James 1:22

This week I will put the lesson into practice by doing the following:

When we are fully trusting God, we can thank Him in every circumstance of life.

Lesson 20

What Paul Said About Prayer

(Part I)

I Thessalonians 5:16-18

In his writings to the Early Church Paul had much to say to these new Christians about prayer. As we have already studied many of his teachings on prayer in several of our previous lessons in this series, we will not repeat them here. We will merely look at some additional things he had to say on prayer in these next two lessons.

I THESSALONIANS 5:16–18

16 Rejoice evermore.

17 Pray without ceasing.

18 In every thing give thanks: for this is the will of God in Christ Jesus concerning you.

Verse 17 in the King James Version is a little misleading as some people have gotten the idea that Paul was telling us here to pray all the time. Other translations of this verse read, "Never give up in prayer," or "Be unceasing in prayer." In other words, don't give up your prayer life. Maintain a prayer life. It doesn't mean that we are to pray with every breath. This is not possible.

The exhortation to never give up in prayer is sandwiched in between the exhortations to "rejoice" and "give thanks." That is a good sandwich, isn't it? Paul said, "Rejoice evermore." We are to be full of rejoicing.

Then he said, "In every thing give thanks: for this is the will of God in Christ Jesus concerning you."

"But I just can't thank God in *everything!*" some might exclaim. Paul said you could. He said this is the will of God in Christ Jesus concerning *you.* We all want to be in the will of God. And we can when we have things in their proper perspective. When we know and act upon the Word of God in this manner, we can truly thank Him in everything.

I have done this in my own life when things looked pretty bleak. When I first started out on the evangelistic field, there were many times that I would close one revival meeting with no other meetings in sight. I had a wife and two children to support. Actually, at the time my niece was also living with us so there were five of us to feed and clothe. When I would close a revival and put the last offering in my pocket, it wouldn't be enough to pay the rent when I got home. I didn't have enough money to buy the food that should be on the table. And I didn't have any prospects for another meeting.

On one such occasion I started driving home after the closing service. I drove at night as my tires were bald and I thought I would have a better chance of making it at night when it was cooler. During the daytime the roads were hot and there was a greater risk of a blowout. And I didn't even have a spare tire.

All the way home the devil perched on my shoulder and whispered in my ear, "What are you going to do now? What are you going to do now?" I didn't have an air conditioner so the windows were rolled down. I could hear the tires singing and it seemed as if the tires picked it up and taunted me—"What are you going to do now? What are you going to do now?" It kept getting louder and louder.

But thank God, when you have the

Word, you can walk in the light of the Word.

I said, "I'll tell you what I am going to do, Mr. Devil. I'm going to act just as if the Word of God is so. I am going to act like the Bible is true. The Bible says, 'Rejoice evermore.' I rejoice for the $42 offering I did get. The Bible says, 'In every thing give thanks . . .' I thank God for the $42. I may have needed $102, but I thank God for the $42. I am rejoicing. I am giving thanks.

"And I'll tell you something else, Mr. Devil. I thank God for this test, for this is just a good time to prove that God is true, and to prove that the Bible is true. This is an opportunity for me to believe God, and I am thanking Him for it. Since you asked me what I'm going to do, I'll tell you exactly what I'm going to do. I am going home and go to bed and sleep like a baby."

I arrived home around two o'clock in the morning and my wife asked, "How did everything go?" I knew she was wondering if I had received enough money to meet the bills.

"Everything is just fine," I told her. "We don't have a thing in the world to worry about. I'll tell you about it in the morning." Then I went to bed and slept soundly and peacefully.

Early the next morning before I had awakened the phone rang. When I answered it the voice on the other end of the line was that of a pastor of whom I had heard but had not actually met. He asked, "When can you start a meeting with us?"

"As soon as you want me to," I answered.

"Then how about starting next Sunday?" he said.

"I'll be there," I said, praising God in my heart for answered prayer, for meeting my needs again as He had in the past because I had trusted in Him. I had obeyed God's Word and had rejoiced in the face of despair. If I had griped all the way home, I am not sure it would have worked out that way.

MEMORY TEXT:

"In every thing give thanks: for this is the will of God in Christ Jesus concerning you." *(I Thess. 5:18)*

THE LESSON IN ACTION: *"But be ye doers of the word, and not hearers only . . ."* James 1:22

This week I will put the lesson into practice by doing the following:

Prayer, accompanied by obedient surrender to God, touches heaven.

Lesson 21

What Paul Said About Prayer
(Part II)

I Timothy 2:1-2, 8; 4:1-5

In Paul's writings to the young minister, Timothy, he had a number of instructions regarding prayer. At this time Timothy was the pastor of a New Testament church.

Pray for Heads of Government

I TIMOTHY 2:1-2

1 I exhort therefore, that, first of all, supplications, prayers, intercessions, and giving of thanks, be made for all men;

2 For kings, and for all that are in authority; that we may lead a quiet and peaceable life in all godliness and honesty.

Too often we put ourselves first in our praying. In fact, sometimes that is as far as we ever get—just praying for ourselves, our own personal lives and needs. But here Paul instructed Timothy, ". . . *First of all,* supplications, prayers, intercessions, and giving of thanks, be made for all men." Then he became more specific and said, "For kings, and for all that are in authority . . . ." In that time the people were ruled by kings. This would be comparable to our president and to the heads of government of our day.

Why did Paul say that we should pray for those in authority? ". . . That we may lead a quiet and peaceable life in all godliness and honesty." Whatever happens in the nation in which we live is

going to affect all of us. God is concerned about us, and whether or not our leaders are Christians, God will do some things for our sake.

We notice that intercession is mentioned here. When Abraham made intercession for Sodom and Gomorrah, God came down and talked with him before destroying those wicked cities. Abraham pleaded to God not to destroy the cities if as many as ten righteous people could be found, and God said, "I will not destroy it for ten's sake" (Gen. 18:32).

There are more than ten righteous people in America so we need not be frightened, but we do need to intercede for our country and for our heads of government. God will do some things just because we ask Him.

Pray With Hands Outstretched to Heaven

I TIMOTHY 2:8

8 I will therefore that men pray every where, lifting up holy hands, without wrath and doubting.

Everyone will agree with the first part of Paul's statement to Timothy—that men everywhere ought to pray. But notice that Paul also gives some explicit instructions on prayer. ". . . Lifting up holy hands, without wrath and doubting."

We would all encourage people to pray without doubting. Jesus said, ". . . Whosoever shall say unto this mountain, Be thou removed, and be thou cast into the sea; and *shall not doubt* in his heart, but shall believe that those things which he saith shall come to pass; he shall have whatsoever he saith" (Mark 11:23). And certainly we can also see the necessity of praying without wrath.

If we encourage people to follow two-thirds of Paul's instructions in this verse, then we should also obey his third admonition: ". . . lifting up holy hands. . . ." Those of us who came from a denominational church background may have found it difficult at first to lift our hands in prayer. I can remember when I first came around folk who lifted their hands to pray. It was the hardest thing I had ever done in my life to lift my hands and pray. Someone may ask, "Do you have to do it?" No, you don't have to do it, but if we are going to obey part of the verse, why not all of it? Why not pray New Testament style?

If Paul was speaking under the inspiration of the Spirit of God in writing to the church, then I am under obligation to obey. If part of it is inspired of God, then all of it is inspired, and we need to pay attention to it.

> According to Hebrews 4:14–16 Jesus is my High Priest. Through Him I can come boldly before the Father's throne where mercy and grace are available to me.

Sanctifying Prayer

I TIMOTHY 4:1–5

1 Now the Spirit speaketh expressly, that in the latter times some shall depart from the faith, giving heed to seducing spirits, and doctrines of devils;

2 Speaking lies in hypocrisy; having their conscience seared with a hot iron;

3 Forbidding to marry, and commanding to abstain from meats, which God hath created to be received with thanksgiving of them which believe and know the truth.

4 And every creature of God is good, and nothing to be refused, if it be received with thanksgiving:

5 For it is sanctified by the word of God and prayer.

In this passage of scripture Paul is not referring to sinners or the heathen world.

He is talking about believers who depart from the faith. Verse 1 says that ". . . some shall depart from the faith, giving heed to seducing spirits, and doctrines of devils."

Then in verse 3 he mentions some of these doctrines of devils. "Forbidding to marry, and commanding to abstain from meats. . . ." Most of us have met individuals who have fallen prey to such erroneous teaching. But Paul, speaking under the inspiration of the Holy Spirit, said concerning meats, ". . . which God hath created to be received with thanksgiving of them which believe and know the truth. And every creature of God is good, and nothing to be refused, if it be received with thanksgiving: For it is sanctified by the word of God and prayer."

The devil will use any means he can to lead people away from God. I once knew a minister who was on fire for God and had a remarkable ministry in reaching the lost. He could get more people saved accidentally than most people can on purpose. But he got off on the subject of diet and started teaching people what to eat and what not to eat. He preached Old Testament dietary laws and spent all of his time trying to regulate people's diets. If he got anyone saved, I don't know of it. The devil simply undermined his spiritual ministry of reaching the lost.

People have asked me, "But do you eat pork?" Certainly I eat pork. I sanctify it "by the word of God and prayer" as Paul teaches. You could eat skunk if you wanted to, for "every creature of God is good, and nothing to be refused, if it be received with thanksgiving" (Verse 4).

We can regulate our diet however we want as long as we receive it with thanksgiving and it is sanctified with prayer. Then nothing we eat need hurt us. Nothing I eat ever hurts me because I sanctify it. I have heard so many people tell me that they can't eat this or they can't eat that because it hurts them if they do. But it need not if you will sanctify it as Paul teaches us in this passage of scripture.

We need to be careful of those segments of the church world which have gone off into these areas, for Paul says that they have given "heed to seducing spirits, and doctrines of devils." ⛨

THE LESSON IN ACTION: *"But be ye doers of the word, and not hearers only..."* James 1:22

This week I will put the lesson into practice by doing the following:

Our prayers are not answered on the basis of how good we have been, but on the basis of our right standing in Christ.

What Others Said About Prayer
(Part I)

James 5:13-18; Jude 20, 21

Let us turn now to some other writers to see what they had to say on the subject of prayer.

What James Said About Prayer

JAMES 5:13-16

13 Is any among you afflicted? let him pray. Is any merry? let him sing psalms.
14 Is any sick among you? let him call for the elders of the church; and let them pray over him, anointing him with oil in the name of the Lord:
15 And the prayer of faith shall save the sick, and the Lord shall raise him up; and if he have committed sins, they shall be forgiven him.
16 Confess your faults one to another, and pray one for another, that ye may be healed. The effectual fervent prayer of a righteous man availeth much.

James asks three questions: "Is any afflicted? . . . Is any merry? . . . Is any sick?" He is talking about three different things here. The words "afflicted" and "sick," as used here, do not mean the same thing. He gave one instruction for the afflicted and quite another for those who were sick.

The Greek word translated here "afflicted" doesn't refer to illness or physical affliction. It means a test or a trial. James said if you are going through a test or trial, do your own praying. Not many do that. Most people go running around to find someone else to do their

praying for them. But James didn't say a word about getting anyone to pray for you in this situation. He said, "Let him pray."

This does not mean that it's not all right for us to pray one for another. The main thing God wants us to learn is to do our own praying. Then we can gain a great victory. But if you have to depend on someone else to pray you out of this trial, then the next time you are confronted with one of life's tests, you won't know the way out. You will have to find someone to pray you out again, and if you can't find someone, you may not make it.

Then James said, "Is any merry? let him sing psalms." This needs little comment. It is easy to sing when we are merry, isn't it?

James then said, "Is any sick among you? let him call for the elders of the church, and let them pray over him . . . ." P. C. Nelson, who was a Greek scholar, brings out the fact in his writings that the Greek word translated "sick" carries with it the thought that the person is so ill he cannot do anything for himself, he is helpless. If a person had a headache or some minor ailment, he could go to the church where the pastor could pray for him. But when he is so ill he cannot get out of bed, he is to call for the elders of the church to pray for him.

We must remember that when James wrote his epistle the church was in its infancy. Disciples would go into a place where there was no church, preach and win people to the Lord, and establish a work. These new churches didn't have all the ministry gifts. Not having a pastor, they would appoint the eldest in the congregation, or in some places those who had matured more spiritually, to be in charge and watch over the flock. As the church developed and grew, God gave "some, apostles; and some, prophets; and some, evangelists; and some, pastors and teachers" (Eph. 4:11). Thus in the process of time there would be those who were separated unto the ministry.

Can a Person With Sin in His Life Be Healed?

James instructed those who were sick to call for the elders to pray for them and anoint them with oil. "And the prayer of faith shall save the sick, and the Lord shall raise him up; and if he have committed sins, they shall be forgiven him" (Verse 15). James was not saying here that everyone is ill because of having committed sins. He was saying the reason *some* are sick is that they have sinned. *"If* he have committed sins, they shall be forgiven him." There is forgiveness and healing for us.

Many have thought that because they have failed God they must continue to be sick, they must pay for their sins. However, this scripture does not say, "If he have committed sins, he has to go on being sick to pay for it." It says, "If he have committed sins, *they shall be forgiven him."*

Then James went on to say, because this is all tied together, "Confess your faults one to another, and pray one for another, that ye may be healed." We dare not take this verse out of its setting and apply it wrongly. James was not suggesting here that we come to church to have a confession meeting. He was saying that when these elders come to pray for the sick man, if he has sinned, he should confess it. He is not going to get healed with unconfessed sin in his life.

> We are the righteousness of God in Him according to II Cor. 5:21.

What Is a 'Righteous' Man?

James followed this admonition with the words, "The effectual fervent prayer of a righteous man availeth much." Then in the next two verses he gave us an example of a righteous man.

JAMES 5:17–18

17 Elias [Elijah] was a man subject to like passions as we are, and he prayed earnestly that it might not rain: and it rained not on the earth by the space of three years and six months.

18 And he prayed again, and the heaven gave rain, and the earth brought forth her fruit.

You might think (and I once thought the same thing), "But Elijah was a prophet. He was a great man of God. I can't possibly do what he did." However, James did not say, "Elijah, who was a prophet, prayed." He said Elijah was a man "subject to like passions as we are." He had the same faults, the same failings, he made the same mistakes we do. Yet his prayer worked.

God won't hear a prophet any more quickly than He will hear any other believer. James didn't say that it was the "effectual fervent prayer of a prophet" that got the job done. He said, "The effectual fervent prayer of a righteous man . . . ."

"Well, if I were righteous I could do it," you might say. But you are righteous, if you are saved, because you are the "righteousness of God in him [Christ]" (II Cor. 5:21). God made you righteous. You cannot make yourself righteous.

While I pastored for nearly twelve years, I often saw people in my congregation who didn't live half as consecrated a life as others did, yet who could pray twice as effectively as the others. They could pray the prayer of faith more quickly for themselves and for their families. I puzzled about this many times until the Lord finally showed me through His

Word that we do not get our prayers answered on the basis of how good we have been and certainly not on the basis of how bad we have been. It is on the basis of our right standing in Him.

We are made righteous in Christ Jesus. "For he hath made him to be sin for us, who knew no sin; that we might be made the righteousness of God in him" (II Cor. 5:21). Righteousness means right standing with God. Jesus is our righteousness. Every single one of us who are born-again believers has the same right standing, the same righteousness that Jesus has. We are invited to come boldly to the throne of grace by way of the blood of Jesus.

What Jude Said About Prayer

Jude also said something about prayer that is enlightening and helpful.

JUDE 20, 21

20 But ye, beloved, building up yourselves on your most holy faith, praying in the Holy Ghost,

21 Keep yourselves in the love of God, looking for the mercy of our Lord Jesus Christ unto eternal life.

Jude's teachings here agree with what Paul said to the church at Corinth. "For if I pray in an unknown tongue, my spirit prayeth . . . ." and "He that speaketh in an unknown tongue edifieth himself" (I Cor. 14:14, 4). (See Lessons 9 and 10.)

The word "edify" means to build up. Praying in an unknown tongue edifies, builds up the believer. It is a means of "spiritual muscle building," so to speak.

Jude did not say here that praying in the Holy Ghost would build your faith. He said, "building up yourselves on your most holy faith." It is foolish to take a text out of its setting and try to prove something with it. We should not try to make a verse say something that doesn't agree with the rest of the Bible by taking it out of its setting. We must interpret it in the light of the whole scripture. We must study it in context, putting all the verses together. Then one will help and modify the other. They will fit together, interpreting one in the light of the other.

Romans 10:17 tells us how to build our faith. "So then faith cometh by hearing, and hearing by the word of God." We build our faith through the study of God's Word. Then through praying in tongues we build up ourselves spiritually on the faith that we already have.

We can build spiritual muscle tone into our everyday lives as we are edified through praying in the Spirit. ⚔

MEMORY TEXT:

". . . The effectual fervent prayer of a righteous man availeth much."

(James 5:16)

THE LESSON IN ACTION: *"But be ye doers of the word, and not hearers only . . ."* James 1:22

This week I will put the lesson into practice by doing the following:

Lesson 23

What Others Said About Prayer
(Part II)

I Peter 3:1-6, 12; I John 5:14-16
Hebrews 6:4-6; Hebrews 10:26-29
III John 2

In Peter's epistles to the church, he too gave them instructions in the matter of prayer.

Relationship to Spouse Can Hinder Prayers

"Likewise, ye husbands, dwell with them according to knowledge, giving honour unto the wife, as unto the weaker vessel, and as being heirs together of the grace of life; *that your prayers be not hindered*" (I Peter 3:7). Here Peter is talking about marriages in which both husband and wife are believers, for he said, ". . . being heirs together of the grace of life . . . ."

Men, if some of your prayers are not being answered, perhaps you should examine your relationship with your wife. Do you show her tenderness and respect, "giving honour unto the wife, as unto the weaker vessel"? If not, Peter says that your prayers are hindered.

He gives similar admonitions to wives. Let us look at them

I Peter 3:1–6

1 Likewise, ye wives, be in subjection to your own husbands; that, if any obey not the word, they also may without the word be won by the conversation of the wives;

2 While they behold your chaste con-versation coupled with fear.

3 Whose adorning let it not be that outward adorning of plaiting the hair, and of wearing of gold, or of putting on of apparel;

4 But let it be the hidden man of the heart, in that which is not corruptible, even the ornament of a meek and quiet spirit, which is in the sight of God of great price.

5 For after this manner in the old time the holy women also, who trusted in God, adorned themselves, being in subjection unto their own husbands:

6 Even as Sara obeyed Abraham, calling him Lord: whose daughters ye are, as long as ye do well, and are not afraid with any amazement.

Here Peter suggests that there is a way of winning an unsaved husband without the Word. ". . . If any obey not the word, they also may without the word be won by the conversation of the wives." The word "conversation" here means one's manner of life, her conduct.

God Hears Prayers of Righteous

Further in this same third chapter, Peter has more to say about prayer.

I Peter 3:12

12 For the eyes of the Lord are over the righteous, and his ears are open unto their prayers: but the face of the Lord is against them that do evil.

Who are the righteous that this verse refers to? In Lesson 22 we saw that we, as born-again believers, are the righteous in Christ Jesus. "For he hath made him to be sin for us, who knew no sin; that we might be made the righteousness of God in him" (II Cor. 5:21). Righteousness is not on the basis of how good or how bad we are, but of our standing in

Christ. Jesus is our righteousness.

Peter said that God's eyes are over us, and "his ears are open unto [our] prayers . . . ." I'm glad that God has eyes and ears, aren't you? He sees us and He hears us. His ears are open to our prayers, but as we saw in verse 7, we can hinder our prayers. God doesn't hinder them, He doesn't refuse to hear. But we can hinder them. Let us take care that we don't hinder them; then we can know that His ears are open unto our prayers.

Watch and Pray

Then in I Peter 4:7 we read, "But the end of all things is at hand: be ye therefore sober, and watch unto prayer." Under the inspiration of the Holy Spirit, Peter saw into the future to the day in which we live and admonished believers concerning the necessity of watchful prayer. In Mark's gospel we read where Jesus,, talking about the last days, said, "Take ye heed, watch and pray: for ye know not when the time is" (Mark 13:33).

God's Will in Prayer

John too had some very important things to say about prayer.

I JOHN 5:14-16

14 And this is the confidence that we have in him, that, if we ask any thing according to his will, he heareth us:

15 And if we know that he hear us, whatsoever we ask, we know that we have the petitions that we desired of him.

16 If any man see his brother sin a sin which is not unto death, he shall ask, and he shall give him life for them that sin not unto death. There is a sin unto death: I do not say that he shall pray for it.

Although the word "pray" is mentioned only once in this passage of scripture, John has used the words "ask" and "petition," referring to prayer. He said, ". . . If we ask any thing according to his will, he heareth us." Remember this: If it is according to the Word, it is according to His will.

Some people take the attitude that they will pray for something and if it is God's will He will give it to them. If it isn't His will, then He won't. However, this isn't what the Bible says. John said, ". . . if we ask any thing according to his will, he heareth us." His Word is His will. If we know what His Word says about a certain matter, then we know what His will is about that matter. This agrees with Jesus' statement, "If ye abide in me and my words abide in you, ye shall ask what ye will, and it shall be done unto you" (John 15:7).

Verse 16 of the above passage has been the subject of much controversy, and most preachers just stay away from it. However, it ties right in with the two preceding verses and continues talking about prayer. John is saying here that if we ask God to forgive someone, this is according to His Word and according to His will, and He will do it.

Several years ago, I was holding a meeting near my home town in Texas and I received a call that my grandmother had fallen into a coma and was near death at her home. Each night after the evening service I drove back to her home and would sit up with her through the night. She never regained consciousness.

The third night as I sat there I prayed, "Dear Lord, I'm so sorry I didn't pray with Granny the other day when I visited her."

I knew Granny was a Christian and loved the Lord, but there are sins of omission as well as commission, and I could see where she had missed it. Others can see where I have missed it. We can see where others miss it sometimes better than we can see ourselves.

So I prayed, "Lord, I wish I had prayed with her. Just let her revive so I can have a word of prayer with her. (She was elderly and I knew in my spirit she was going to go.) Let me make sure there isn't any unconfessed sin in her life."

As I prayed Someone said, "Why don't you ask me to forgive her?"

It was so real it startled me. I jumped out of the chair and the Bible on my lap scooted across the floor and under the bed.

"Who said that?" I asked. I thought someone had heard me praying and was teasing me. However, I found no one when I looked around the room and outside the door. I sat back down and began to study but I couldn't concentrate so I started to pray again.

"Lord, why don't you bring her out of it and let me have a word of prayer with her to see that she doesn't die with any unconfessed sin in her life?"

Again that Voice said, "Why don't you ask me to forgive her?"

I jumped again and said, "Someone is playing tricks on me." But a check into the bedrooms of everyone else in the house revealed they were soundly sleeping.

I went back to her bedroom and tried to study but I could not so I began again to pray. When I did, the third time He said, "Why don't you ask me to forgive her?"

This time I had presence of mind to remember the child Samuel and that Eli told Samuel to answer when God called. I realized it was the Lord and I answered, "Me ask you?"

He said, "Yes, you ask me. Don't you know that my Word says in I John 5:16, 'If any man see his brother sin a sin which is not unto death, he shall ask, and he shall give him life for them . . . .'?"

I turned the pages of my Bible to that scripture and read it. "That's right. That's exactly what it says! All right, Lord, I ask you. Please forgive her. You forgive her of these things that I can see of omission, and of anything else that she didn't see or I don't see, You forgive her."

He said, "All right, I have."

So I thanked Him for it. To me that settled it. Can't you see that this was according to His will?

The last part of that verse does make an exception, however. It says, ". . . There is a sin unto death: I do not say that he shall pray for it." How will we know if they have committed this sin unto death? *We will only know this as the Holy Spirit reveals it to us.* This has happened to me only two times in my life when I have been praying for someone and the Lord showed me that there was no need to pray for them, that they had sinned the sin unto death.

What is this sin unto death? First of all, John is not talking about physical death here but about spiritual death. This isn't a sin that an unbeliever can commit. It is a sin only a Christian can commit, for he used the term "brother."

Let us look into the book of Hebrews to find out more about this.

HEBREWS 6:4–6

4 For it is impossible for those who were once enlightened, and have tasted of the heavenly gift, and were made partakers of the Holy Ghost,

5 And have tasted the good word of God, and the powers of the world to come,

6 If they shall fall away, to renew them again unto repentance; seeing they crucify to themselves the Son of God afresh, and put him to an open shame.

HEBREWS 10:26–29

26 For if we sin wilfully after that we have received the knowledge of the truth, there remaineth no more sacrifice for sins.

27 But a certain fearful looking for of judgment and fiery indignation, which shall devour the adversaries.

28 He that despised Moses' law died without mercy under two or three witnesses:

29 Of how much sorer punishment, suppose ye, shall he be thought worthy, who hath trodden under foot the Son of God, and hath counted the blood of the covenant, wherewith he was sanctified, an

unholy thing, and hath done despite unto the Spirit of grace?

The sin God is talking about here is not the sin of lying, cheating or something like that. God offers forgiveness for such sins. There is no forgiveness, however, for those who have "trodden under foot the Son of God . . . ."

The Hebrew Christians, to which this book was written, were under great persecution and were tempted to go back to Judaism. When they accepted Christ they were cut off from their families, ran into financial hardships, and faced numerous other trials. But God warned them in these scriptures that to go back to Judaism was to deny Christ. It was to say that "the blood of the covenant, wherewith he was sanctified, is an unholy thing," or in other words that Jesus' blood was just common blood like any other man's.

Let us remember that as long as a person stays in Christ, he is eternally secure. But we don't want to forget that there is a sin unto death.

John's Three-Dimensional Prayer

III JOHN 2:2

2 Beloved, I wish above all things that thou mayest prosper and be in health, even as thy soul prospereth.

The word which is translated "wish" in the King James Version is "pray" in the original Greek. Therefore, John said here, "Beloved, I *pray* above all things that thou mayest prosper and be in health, even as thy soul prospereth." If he was motivated by the Spirit to pray that way, then that would be the desire of the Spirit of God for every person. It is all right, then, to pray for financial prosperity, for John said, "I pray above all things . . . ."

John's prayer here concerned three dimensions of our lives—physical, spiritual, and material. He said, ". . . I pray . . . that thou mayest prosper (material blessing) and be in health (physical blessing), even as thy soul prospereth (spiritual blessing)." God desires to bless every part of the believer's life. ⚔

MEMORY TEXT:

"For the eyes of the Lord are over the righteous, and his ears are open unto their prayers: but the face of the Lord is against them that do evil."

(I Peter 3:12)

THE LESSON IN ACTION: *"But be ye doers of the word, and not hearers only..."* James 1:22

This week I will put the lesson into practice by doing the following:

Lesson 24

The Will of God
in Prayer
(Part I)

John 3:16; II Peter 3:9; Acts 16:31

In these next three lessons we will focus our attention on the will of God in prayer. As we look at our memory text in I John 5:14 we want to emphasize two words: "confidence" and "heareth." "And this is the *confidence* that we have in him, that, if we ask anything according to his will, he *heareth* us." Another translation of this verse says, "And this is the boldness we have toward him . . . ." Under what condition can we have confidence that God heareth us when we pray? (He hears us if we ask anything according to His will.)

In the next verse we read, "And if we know that he hear us, whatsoever we ask, we know that we have the petitions that we desired of him." As this scripture says, "And if . . . he hear us . . . we have the petitions that we desired . . ." it would seem that there must be something that He doesn't hear. If when we pray we do not have this confidence, this boldness, then it must follow that the Lord doesn't hear us. If we do not fulfill our part, then it won't work.

How can we get this confidence, this boldness, this faith? The Word of God gives faith. "So then faith cometh by hearing, and hearing by the word of God" (Rom. 10:17). "The entrance of thy words giveth light . . ." (Psalm 119:130). "Thy word is a lamp unto my feet, and a light unto my path" (Psalm 119:105). When we walk in the light of the

Word, we are not walking in darkness.

Many times when we pray we pray in darkness. We don't know what God's will is and we are just praying in the dark. We don't come with confidence or boldness. We come trembling and fearful, yet hoping that He will hear us. But that won't work. We can go to the Word and find out what His Word says about our particular problem, and then pray in faith, knowing His will in the matter. Almost everything that we need to pray about is covered in His Word.

The Will of God Concerning Salvation

We know first of all that saving the lost is His will, for it is to this end that Jesus came and died.

JOHN 3:16

16 For God so loved the world, that he gave his only begotten Son, that whosoever believeth in him should not perish, but have everlasting life.

II PETER 3:9

9 The Lord is not slack concerning his promise, as some men count slackness; but is longsuffering to usward, not willing that any should perish, but that all should come to repentance.

ACTS 16:31

31 And they said, Believe on the Lord Jesus Christ, and thou shalt be saved, and thy house.

I know of no one who would pray for a lost loved one and say, "Lord, if it is your will save him." On the other hand, much of our praying for the lost is not effective, not because we question the will of God in it but because we do not come with confidence and boldness.

Our scripture says that if we come with

confidence and boldness, asking according to His will, then we know that He hears us and that we have the petitions we desire. That should settle that case for victory and close it out. However, our praying in this realm is too often in the natural instead of in the spirit. It is entirely in the mental or physical realm. We pray, "God save our loved one," and then we wait to see if God has answered our prayer. If they get saved immediately, we believe He heard us. If they don't, or if we see no change in their lives, we think that He didn't hear us. This is walking by sight and not by faith, which only brings confusion.

One might say, "I have prayed and prayed for my unsaved loved ones and it seems as if my praying doesn't work." But if you will come right back to God's Word, it will enlighten you. God's Word will instruct you as to why your prayers are not answered. "And this is the confidence that we have in him, that, if we ask anything according to his will . . . ." There is no question but that it is His will to save the lost, as we have seen from the scriptures above. The Word is His will, and if it is according to His will, then we know that we have the petitions that we desired of Him.

I once knew a country preacher who, because of his limited education, never had an opportunity to pastor a very large church. Most of his pastorates were small community churches. However, he was in constant demand to hold revivals because of his tremendous success in soul winning. Wherever he would go, a landslide of souls would follow. He would often go to a church where no one had been saved for years, and he would see great numbers accept Christ as Saviour.

When he was in his early sixties and still having phenomenal success, I once asked him the secret of his success. "It is a very simple thing," he told me. "I just apply the same faith to see folks saved as you do to see folks healed or to believe God for anything. It never enters my mind to doubt that people will come to be saved. If the doubt did come, I would resist it in the name of Jesus. I pray, but not more than others do. I do seek God, of course, but I attribute my success in soul winning to one thing—I just have confidence that they will come. By the eye of faith I see the altar filling up with lost souls. If the meeting is not going as well as it should, I don't necessarily increase my praying about it. I just exercise more faith."

This preacher was expressing the confidence, the boldness, that our scripture is talking about, because He knew the will of God in the matter.

But some folks can only look to the circumstances. They say, "No one came to the altar for salvation last night, they probably won't tonight either." This kind of person is looking at the wrong thing. He may pray for lost souls, but he does not see them coming to Christ. He does not really have confidence that they will come. His faith is only in what he can see.

We Can Nullify Our Prayers

Often times people undo their prayers. They have prayed and solicited the help of others in praying, but then they nullify their prayers and the faith of those who are praying with them by speaking negatively. Talk faith, not doubt.

I once knew a minister who asked me as well as others to pray for his son. But at the same time he was praying and requesting prayer, he would tell his boy, "You'll never amount to anything. I don't know what in the world I'm going to do with you. I have done everything I can do. I have prayed and prayed, but it looks as though my prayers didn't do any good."

This man was confessing defeat and failure rather than victory and faith. He was building doubt and insecurity into his son. And this is where so many people have lost their children.

As we pray for our children, we must not do anything in the home that would nullify the effects of our prayers. We must build confidence and trust in our children. We must instill in them a sense of security.

As a young man traveling on the evangelistic field, before I was married I usually stayed in the home of the pastor during my revival meetings. I often felt sorry for the children in the homes where I stayed. In one home in particular there was a twelve-year-old boy. His parents were impatient and short-tempered with him and were always telling him that he would never amount to anything. Sure enough, he didn't. Today he is forty years old and has broken the hearts of his parents. He has been married several times and has never provided a living for his family.

These parents may have prayed and asked the church to pray. They may have shed many tears and done much fasting, but their lives nullified the effects of their prayers. From the spiritual standpoint as well as the natural standpoint the things that happen to children in their early years are what mold their lives as adults. Let these be spiritually rich and meaningful years in which our life witness will match our words. Let's not work against God, let's work with Him.

In many of the pastor's homes where I have stayed, I have seen the children neglected. The pastors' wives were so busy working in the church that the children were left alone to do as they pleased. For that reason, when I married I told my wife, "I'll run the church and you run the house." I would never allow my wife to teach Sunday School. In the first church we pastored after we were married we were told it was their custom for the pastor to teach the adult Bible class of men and the pastor's wife to teach the

women. I told them that my wife didn't teach Sunday School. They argued, "But it is our custom here. We have been doing this for more than twenty years."

"Well, I just changed that custom. We'll consolidate the two classes and make one big auditorium class, and I will teach it. My wife doesn't teach Sunday School."

When they asked me why, I told them, "I am going to preach and pastor the church; my wife is going to stay home and keep house, take care of me and the children. I want her to run things there and I'll run things here. There are many capable people in the church who can work, so let's put them to work." When they wanted to make my wife president of the women's missionary council I again put my foot down. "She can attend the meetings," I told them, "but she won't serve in any capacity." And this has paid off well for us.

Authority to Claim Family for Christ

Every believer has authority in his own household. We have more authority there than we do anywhere else. "Believe on the Lord Jesus Christ, and thou shalt be saved, *and thy house*" (Acts 16:31). But too many people, in praying for their household, have struggled and begged God to save them, and have not backed up their prayers by claiming the promise. They have prayed in darkness instead of the light of God's Word.

Our scripture text says, ". . . if we ask anything according to his will . . . ." We know that salvation for our children is His will. ". . . He heareth us: And if we know that he hear us . . . we know that we have the petitions that we desired of him" (I John 5:14-15). Then if we know He heard us, we don't have to keep begging him to save our children. This doesn't mean that overnight the whole family will come to Christ, but as we stand in faith, thanking God, they will come.

For us to go on asking and begging God is a confession that we don't believe we have the petition. If we really believed that we had the petition that we desired of the Lord, as the scripture says, we would be thanking Him for it. Sometimes we go through the right motions but without the right believing. We can go through all the motions just because someone told us to do it or because someone else did it. But we must have faith down in our hearts for it to work.

The thought never entered my mind that my immediate family would not be saved, for I have authority and power there. I prayed for them once and claimed their salvation on the basis of the Word. When the thought would come to me that they might not be saved, I would immediately reject it in the name of Jesus. For I had confidence, I had boldness that they would be saved because I had prayed according to His will.

Knowing what the will of God is concerning lost souls, we need never pray, "Lord, if it be your will, save this one, or that one." We know it is His will.

MEMORY TEXT:

"And this is the confidence that we have in him, that, if we ask anything according to his will, he heareth us: And if we know that he hear us, whatsoever we ask, we know that we have the petitions that we desired of him." *(I John 5:14–15)*

THE LESSON IN ACTION: *"But be ye doers of the word, and not hearers only..."* James 1:22

This week I will put the lesson into practice by doing the following:

Lesson 25

The Will of God in Prayer
(Part II)

Isaiah 53:4,5; Matthew 8:16-17
I Peter 2:24

As we continue our study about God's will in prayer, let us look at these pertinent words of Jesus in John 15:7: "If ye abide in me, and my words abide in you, ye shall ask what ye will, and it shall be done unto you." Under what conditions did Jesus tell us to ask what we will? He said, "If ye abide in me . . . ." In other words, to be born again is the first requirement. If we are born again, then we are abiding in Him.

Then He also said, ". . . and my words abide in you." So we must have a thorough knowledge of God's Word to be an effective prayer warrior. We must have His Word abiding in us. In order to do this we must, "Study to show thyself approved unto God, a workman that needeth not to be ashamed, rightly dividing the word of truth" (II Tim. 2:15).

When we have God's Word abiding in us, then we know what His will is concerning any matter about which we need to pray. For as we saw in our last lesson, God's Word is His will. Therefore, we can come with confidence and boldness to God's throne of grace with our petitions.

If we have followed steps one and two of the above verse—if we are (1) abiding in Him, and (2) His Word abides in us —then we can "ask what ye will, and it shall be done unto you." What a powerful promise!

The believer walking in fellowship with the Word will never ask for anything outside of the will of God. If he knows the Word, then he knows what is promised him. He knows the will of God. If he is not walking in fellowship with the Word, he is not going to have a successful prayer life and get answers to his prayers anyhow. His prayer life isn't going to be effective, because Jesus plainly stated, "If ye abide in me, and my words abide in you . . . ." We must come according to His conditions.

God's Will Concerning Healing

What does God's Word have to say about physical healing? Is it His will to heal the sick? Let us look at some scripture to determine His will in this matter.

ISAIAH 53:4–5

4 Surely he hath borne our griefs, and carried our sorrows: yet we did esteem him stricken, smitten of God, and afflicted.

5 But he was wounded for our transgressions, he was bruised for our iniquities: the chastisement of our peace was upon him; and with his stripes we are healed.

MATTHEW 8:16–17

16 When the even was come, they brought unto him many that were possessed with devils: and he cast out the spirits with his word, and healed all that were sick:

17 That it might be fulfilled which was spoken by Esaias the prophet, saying, Himself took our infirmities, and bare our sicknesses.

I PETER 2:24

24 Who his own self bare our sins in his own body on the tree, that we, being dead to sins, should live unto righteousness: by whose stripes ye were healed.

We see from the above verses that healing the sick is God's will because Christ bore our infirmities and carried our diseases. Just as He purchased our salvation through His death on the cross, so He has purchased our healing. "... By whose stripes ye were healed." When we have His Word firmly settled in our hearts, then we need not wonder if it is His will to heal us. We need not pray, "Lord, heal me ... if it be thy will."

Years ago while pastoring a church I was called to pray for one of the members who was ill. I went to her bedside to pray for her, knowing the importance of her own confession of faith for healing I asked her, "Sister, will you be healed now as I anoint you with oil and lay hands on you in Jesus' name?"

"Well, I will if it's God's will," she answered.

"How are you going to find out whether it is His will?" I asked.

"I thought you would pray for me, and if it's His will, I'll be healed. If it isn't, then I won't."

Under these circumstances I knew the woman was not going to receive healing. I knew her unbelief would stop the flow of God's healing power. I wanted to talk to her and show her some things from the Word of God before I prayed for her, but she said, "Go ahead and pray for me. I am in so much pain and misery." I anointed her and prayed, knowing in my heart that she wouldn't receive anything because she wasn't believing in line with the Word. I stumbled through a prayer and hardly said "amen" when she said to her husband, "Pete, go call the doctor."

The thing that really puzzled me, though, was that she had just gotten through saying that if it was God's will for her to be healed, He would heal her and if it wasn't then He wouldn't. She didn't get healed; therefore, by her own admission it wasn't God's will for her to be healed. Yet here she was calling the doctor and paying him to get her out of the will of God. It would seem, according to her reasoning, that she wouldn't even want to get well then, for she would be getting out of God's will. It would be wrong to buy medicine and enlist the help of the doctor to get her out of the will of God.

Certainly, this is a foolish line of reasoning, but this is the logic that some people follow concerning prayer for their healing.

As we have said before, if we want to know God's will concerning a matter, look to His Word. His Word is His will. His Word tells us that it is His will to heal us. Let us not doubt His Word, but instead claim its promises for our healing.

Look to the Word for God's Will

In similar situations this is the conclusion which people reach many times. They try to find the will of God by saying, "If it's His will He'll do it and if it is not His will, He won't." But we should determine His will in the matter by looking into the Word. I find the answer for anything I might pray for in the Word. If I am uncertain about something, I go to the Word first. I don't just pray uncertainly for I would be wasting my time. I could not pray in faith. I would be praying in unbelief and doubt and it wouldn't work. When we know what God's Word says about a matter, then we know what His will is.

Many times people want to put all the responsibility for a matter on God so they say, "It must not have been God's will, because I prayed, 'If it be thy will, do this ...' and He didn't do it. Therefore, it must not be His will." These people want to relieve themselves of all responsibility and put it all on God. But we don't get out that easily. God has given us His Word and told us to "Search the scriptures ... which testify of me" (John 5:39). In them we learn His will.

Then there are those who know what God's Word says about a matter, yet find it hard to believe that it will work in their case. They are like the man who knew he was going to be needing some extra money so he went to his banker to arrange a loan. He did not need the money right away but just wanted to have everything ready so that he would have access to it when he did need it.

The man filled out all the forms and handed them to the banker. Seeing that everything was in order, the banker told him he could have the money, to come in anytime he wanted and pick it up. The man had his banker's word for it, but then he thought, "What if he doesn't give it to me? What if he didn't mean what he said?" The man will have to believe what the banker said and act on it in order to get his money.

Some people are just like that with God. They know what He said about healing, salvation for their loved ones, or any other need they might have, but they find it hard to believe that He will do what He said He would do. But thank God, He keeps His Word! ⛨

MEMORY TEXT:

"If ye abide in me, and my words abide in you, ye shall ask what ye will, and it shall be done unto you."
(John 15:7)

THE LESSON IN ACTION: *"But be ye doers of the word, and not hearers only..."* James 1:22

This week I will put the lesson into practice by doing the following:

We can find a promise in God's Word for every aspect of life.
Then we can know how to pray, and we can have the assurance
before we pray what His will is.

Lesson 26

The Will of God
in Prayer

(Part III)

I Peter 5:7; III John 2
Philippians 4:19

Studying God's Word is like searching for valuable gems. We can find a few jewels on top of the ground without much digging. But if we really want to get down where the valuable veins are, we have to dig for them. If we just go along on the surface we may pick up a small diamond occasionally, but if we will dig down a little deeper we will find large gems and jewels. To learn the deeper truths of God, we are told to "Search the scriptures; for in them ye think ye have eternal life: and they are they which testify of me" (John 5:39).

Surface reading of our memory text in I John 5:14-15 has brought some to the wrong conclusion of what John was saying here. He said, "And this is the confidence that we have in him, that, if we ask any thing according to his will, he heareth us: And if we know that he hear us: whatsoever we ask, we know that we have the petitions that we desired of him." Some have thought John said, "If it is His will, He will hear me and if it isn't, He won't." However, that wasn't what he meant at all. John was saying that if we have God's Word on a matter, we don't have to say, "If it be thy will," because we know His Word is His will.

For this reason I encourage folks to find scriptures pertaining to their particular need when they pray. Find scriptures with a promise concerning what you are praying about. Sometimes when people ask me to pray for them I ask them, "What scripture are you standing on?" Many times they answer that they have none in particular. "Well," I tell them, "that is what you'll get then, nothing in particular."

If it is according to His Word, then that is His will. It has to be His will for Him to promise it in His Word. It is His will that we have everything He has provided for us in His Word. I have found in my own experience that I can find a promise in His Word for every aspect of life. Then we can know just how to pray, and we can have the assurance before we pray as to what His will is.

Many times the reason prayer isn't working for people is that they are praying in darkness. They are trying to get God to help them apart from the Word. The Psalmist said, "The entrance of thy words giveth light" (Psalm 119:130), and again "Thy word is a lamp unto my feet, and a light unto my path" (Psalm 119:105). We are to walk in the light of the Word. No one can build a successful prayer life if he doesn't know the Word. A successful prayer life is built and based upon the written Word of God. When we pray according to the Word, the Word is a lamp unto our feet and a light unto our path. We know then which way we are walking. Too much of the time, because of a failure to see what God's Word has to say about a subject, we stumble about not knowing just where we are going. Prayer then becomes a matter of desperation, of begging God to do something. But when we know the Word ahead of time, we can come to God with confidence.

93

God's Will Concerning Worry

I PETER 5:7

7 Casting all your care upon him; for he careth for you.

A woman with a look of desperation on her face came to me once requesting prayer. She began crying as she said, "Brother Hagin, the cares of life, the anxieties and worries are just so great." She began to cry harder as she said, "I just can't carry all my burdens. I want you to pray that God will do one of two things—that He will either give me grace to carry them or else take about half of them away. I can carry half of them, but I just can't carry them all."

"Well, I just can't pray that prayer," I told her. "It would be unscriptural." A bewildered look came across her face, and I went on to explain, "I cannot pray for you out of the will of God. If I am going to have any confidence that God will hear my prayer, I must pray in line with the Word of God. The Bible tells us, 'And this is the confidence that we have in him, that, if we ask any thing according to his will, he heareth us: And if we know that he hear us: whatsoever we ask, we know that we have the petitions that we desired of him.'

"I know God's will for you because I know what God's Word says. It isn't His will to give you grace to bear your load of care. Nor is it His will to take half of it away and let you carry the other half. How do I know this? Because of what His Word says. I Peter 5:7 says, 'Casting all your care upon him; for he careth for you.' That verse doesn't say to cast half of your cares, it says *all*. That verse doesn't say that God will give you grace to carry your worries, it says to cast *all* your care upon Him. Why? Because 'He careth for you.' "

Then I said, "Sister, isn't it wonderful that we already have the answer for your prayer right here?" Then I read her this same verse from the Amplified New Testament, which is more explicit. "Casting the whole of your care—all your anxieties, all your worries, all your concerns, for He cares for you affectionately, and cares about you watchfully."

God's Will Concerning Financial Blessing

III JOHN 2:2

2 Beloved, I wish above all things that thou mayest prosper and be in health, even as thy soul prospereth.

PHILIPPIANS 4:19

19 But my God shall supply all your need according to his riches in glory by Christ Jesus.

In Paul's letter to the church at Philippi, he was commending the Christians for their generosity in giving, as we see from the verses just preceding this one. They had made up an offering of money and goods to send to other Christians, and because of this Paul was saying to them, "Because you have given to them and helped them, God shall supply all your need." He was talking about material and financial matters.

Another verse which we think of in connection with financial blessing is found in Luke 6:38. "Give, and it shall be given unto you; good measure, pressed down, and shaken together, and running over, shall men give into your bosom. For with the same measure that ye mete withal it shall be measured to you again." We usually hear this verse quoted when an offering is being taken and the emphasis is usually on the first part of the verse—"give." But let us not overlook the results of that giving—"and it shall be given unto you . . ." We see financial blessings promised in this verse.

Would you like to see increased financial blessings in your life? Then increase your giving, for the scripture says that your returns will be "pressed down, and shaken together, and running over . . . For with the same measure that ye mete withal it shall be measured to you again."

We can hinder our prayers for financial prosperity by not cooperating with God. We can hinder our prayers by not entering into the doors that God opens for us. I knew a young able-bodied fellow who was without work for quite some time. He had a wife and five children. Folks in the church they attended helped them out by taking them groceries and clothes for the children. The church women also helped all they could by giving ironing and other work to his wife so she could earn a little money. When I talked to the man he told me, "Well, the Lord said He would meet all of our needs. Some folk tell me to get out and look for a job, but I am just waiting for the right one to come to me. The Lord will do it. And in the meantime we are getting along all right."

But someone else was paying his house rent and feeding his family. We can't just sit down and wait for something to come to us. The only thing that will come will be a pile of bills. A man can believe that God will help him and bless him financially, but then he needs to move in the right direction and do whatever his hand finds to do. If the first job he finds isn't exactly what he prefers to do, at least it will help him until something better comes along. In the meantime he can pray for guidance and help toward getting a better job. God can open another door for him and another job for him as he is faithful in whatever he finds to do in providing for his family.

As we continue to dig deeper into God's Word we will see more and more things showing us His will in prayer. For example, we know to pray for the lost in heathen lands, for His Word says, "Ask of me, and I shall give thee the heathen for thine inheritance, and the uttermost parts of the earth for thy possession" (Psalm 2:8). Then we know to pray that God would send forth ministers in the power of His Spirit. "Pray ye therefore the Lord of the harvest, that he will send forth labourers into his harvest" (Matt. 9:38).

As we study the Word of God, instead of saying "according to the will of God," we will say "according to the Word of God." Then we will have it in the right focus. ⚔

MEMORY TEXT:

"And this is the confidence that we have in him, that, if we ask any thing according to his will, he heareth us: And if we know that he hear us: whatsoever we ask, we know that we have the petitions that we desired of him." *(I John 5:14-15)*

THE LESSON IN ACTION: *"But be ye doers of the word, and not hearers only..."* James 1:22

This week I will put the lesson into practice by doing the following: